Case Studies in Rational Emotive Behavior Therapy with Children and Adolescents

Albert Ellis

of The Albert Ellis Institute

Jerry Wilde

Indiana University East

D1455910

Upper Saddle River, New Jersey
Columbus, Ohio

Library of Congress Cataloging in Publication Data

Ellis, Albert.
    Case studies in rational emotive behavior therapy with children and adolescents / Albert
Ellis, Jerry Wilde.
        p. cm.
    Includes bibliographical references.
    ISBN 0-13-087281-4
        1. Child psychotherapy—Case studies. 2. Adolescent psychotherapy—Case studies. 3.
Rational-emotive psychotherapy—Case studies. I. Wilde, Jerry. II. Title.

RJ505.R33 E44 2002
618.92′89142—dc21

2001044990

Vice President and Publisher: Jeffery W. Johnston
Executive Editor: Kevin M. Davis
Associate Editor: Christina M. Tawney
Editorial Assistant: Autumn Crisp
Production Editor: Mary Harlan
Production Coordination: Cliff Kallemeyn, Clarinda Publication Services
Design Coordinator: Diane C. Lorenzo
Cover Design: Thomas Mack
Cover Art: SuperStock
Production Manager: Laura Messerly
Director of Marketing: Ann Castel Davis
Marketing Manager: Amy June
Marketing Coordinator: Barbara Koontz

This book was set in Garamond Light by The Clarinda Company. It was printed and bound by Maple Vail
Book Manufacturing Group. The cover was printed by The Lehigh Press, Inc.

Pearson Education Ltd., *London*
Pearson Education Australia Pty. Limited, *Sydney*
Pearson Education Singapore Pte. Ltd.
Pearson Education North Asia Ltd., *Hong Kong*
Pearson Education Canada, Ltd., *Toronto*
Pearson Educación de Mexico, S.A. de C.V., *Mexico*
Pearson Education—Japan, *Tokyo*
Pearson Education Malaysia Pte. Ltd.
Pearson Education, *Upper Saddle River, New Jersey*

10 9 8 7 6 5 4 3 2 1
ISBN: 0-13-087281-4

To the memory of Howard Young, who was one of the best supervisors I (AE) ever trained in REBT and one of the therapists I (JW) never actually knew but always greatly admired.

PREFACE

Case Studies in Rational Emotive Behavior Therapy with Children and Adolescents was written to give readers insight into the authentic workings of REBT with school-aged populations. Casebooks are excellent learning tools, but there is a significant difference between describing therapeutic interventions and showing exactly how experienced therapists use precise language, analogies, and other "tricks of the trade" to bring about a therapeutic result. Readers of this text will feel as though they have a "ringside seat" on treating children by reading verbatim sessions focusing on a wide range of problems facing children and adolescents today.

The idea for this project came from *Growth Through Reason* (Ellis, 1971), also a casebook of verbatim transcripts of REBT sessions, albeit with adult clients. As a young therapist I (JW) found *Growth Through Reason* to be an invaluable resource and learned much from the cases Ellis and other therapists presented. I read and reread cases and found that being able to pick apart the therapist's language was critical to my development. I could place myself into the session and think, "How would I have responded to that statement by the client?" It was as if I had six different tutors helping me learn different applications of REBT. The book also shattered one of my misconceptions about REBT, namely that REBT had to be done the way Albert Ellis did it! There are numerous ways to use REBT, and the strength of *Case Studies in Rational Emotive Behavior Therapy with Children and Adolescents* lies in offering the reader an opportunity to glean from the styles of several experienced therapists.

My only disappointment with *Growth Through Reason* had to do with the fact that of the six cases, only one was with an adolescent and none were with children. *Case Studies in Rational Emotive Behavior Therapy with Children and Adolescents* is designed to provide child and adolescent therapists the same type of inside perspective that is so valuable.

The subject matter in these case studies is varied to give readers glimpses into sessions on anger management, peer pressure, self-esteem issues, bed-wetting, perfectionism, and weight control. Following each case there is insightful discussion of the sessions. Albert Ellis and I give our frank reactions to the sessions, which may clarify issues or help the reader think about the choices the therapists made during the session.

Psychotherapy is a difficult undertaking, and therapy with children and adolescents presents additional roadblocks. *Case Studies in Rational Emotive Behavior Therapy with Children and Adolescents* will allow novice and seasoned professionals alike to learn from the skills of experienced REBT therapists. This text will help its readers fully learn REBT and give new and experienced therapists some new ideas to consider.

Jerry Wilde, Ph.D.

I am very happy that this book includes a number of verbatim case studies that honestly present several unique ways REBT can be done. It is, I think, a splendid addition to the professional literature.

Albert Ellis, Ph.D.

ACKNOWLEDGMENTS

The authors would like to thank the therapists who contributed to this book because without you, the book would not have been possible. By sharing your skills with the next generation of therapists, you have allowed helpers to do a better job of helping. Readers of this book will most likely never know you or the clients you have helped but will know that your contributions are sincerely appreciated.

Michelle Young allowed us to use her husband's work in the book and for that we are grateful; we also know this book is better because of Howard Young's transcript. His ability to disarm even the most resistant clients could never be appreciated without using an actual transcript from him. His session is a great way to start this book.

Christina Tawney from Merrill Education provided a great deal of support and encouragement throughout this project.

We also thank those who reviewed this manuscript: John P. Anderson, Wake Forest University; Kevin A Fall, Loyola University, New Orleans; Chet H. Fischer, Radford University; John J. Horan, Arizonia State University; and Ed Jacobs, West Virginia University.

CONTRIBUTORS

Albert Ellis has M.A and Ph.D. degrees in Clinical Psychology from Columbia University. He is the founder of Rational Emotive Behavior Therapy (REBT), the pioneering form of the modern Cognitive Behavior therapies. He is the president of the Albert Ellis Institute in New York, where he practices individual and group psychotherapy, supervises and trains psychotherapists, and presents many talks and workshops at the Institute and throughout the world. He has published over seven hundred articles and more than sixty books on psychotherapy, marital and family therapy, and sex therapy.

Marie Joyce has Master of Educational Psychology and Ph.D. degrees from the University of Melbourne, Australia. She is a clinical and academic psychologist at Australian Catholic University, where she is responsible for postgraduate training programs in Clinical Psychology and Educational and Developmental Psychology. She has published in the area of REBT since 1984.

Terry London has been an active educator and psychotherapist in the Chicago area for the last 25 years. His private practice includes individual, family, and group work. He has an M.S. in Counseling Psychology and is a certified Rational Emotive Behavior Therapist and an Associate Fellow of the Albert Ellis Institute. He has taught at Triton College, Governor's State University, and Illinois Renewal Institute, Inc. (Saint Xavier College). He has written a number of books relating to REBT and is co-director, with Paul Hauck, of the Chicago Institute for Rational Emotive Behavior Therapy.

Rod Martel is a licensed psychologist working as a Special Educator in The Minneapolis Public School System. He earned a B.A. degree from Northeastern Illinois University, a B.S. from the University of Minnesota, and an M.A. in Educational Psychology from the University of Minnesota. He holds Associate Fellow and Supervisor Certificates from The Albert Ellis Institute. He has over 20 years experience as a specialist in the areas of school-based violence prevention programs as well as the delivery of services to emotionally disturbed/behaviorally disordered, learning disabled, and mild/moderate mentally impaired populations.

Tom Mooney received his M.A. and Ed.D. degrees from Western Michigan University in Counseling Psychology. He has been on the Psychology staff at St. Clair County Community College for the past 36 years. A fully licensed psychologist, he has been in private practice in Port Huron, Michigan, for the past 25 years. He is a founding member of the Society for the Psychological Study of Men and Masculinity. His chapter, "Cognitive Behavior Therapy and the Male Issues," was recently published in Pollack and Lavant's *New Psychotherapy for Men*.

Ann Vernon received her M.A. and Ph.D. degrees from the University of Iowa. She is a professor and coordinator of the Counseling program at the University of Northern Iowa. In addition to teaching, she has a private practice specializing in work with children, adolescents, and parents. She is director of the Midwest Center for Rational Emotive Behavior Therapy and on the board of trustees for the Albert Ellis Institute. She is the author of numerous books and articles, including *Thinking, Feeling, Behaving* and The Passport Programs—emotional education programs for children and adolescents based on REBT.

Jerry Wilde earned his bachelor's degree from Luther College and his Ph.D. from Marquette University. He currently serves as an assistant professor of Educational Psychology for Indiana University East. Prior to this appointment, he had ten years of experience counseling children who had emotional, behavioral, and learning difficulties. He has written twelve books on such topics as psychotherapy with children, parenting, and educational issues. He presents workshops on such subjects as anger management and cognitive-behavior therapy with children and adolescents.

Howard Young received a bachelor's degree from Rutgers University and a Master's of Social Work from Smith College School for Social Work. He worked at the Hibbard Psychiatric Clinic in Huntington, West Virginia. His publications include the best selling "A Rational Counseling Primer" (Institute for Rational Emotive Therapy, 1974). He died at age 46.

CONTENTS

INTRODUCTION

Basic Theoretical Formulations of
Rational Emotive Behavior Therapy

Rational Emotive Behavior Therapy (REBT) is based on the theory that emotional disturbance is largely the result of illogical and irrational patterns of thinking (Ellis, 1962, 1994). Such ideas date back to ancient Asian philosophy and particularly to the first century AD when the Stoic philosopher Epictetus wrote, "People are disturbed not by things but by the views they take of them." In other words, it is not external events alone that cause emotional disturbance, but those events plus a person's perceptions and evaluations about them, as many ancient and modern philosophers have stated.

I (AE), the originator of REBT, was originally trained in Rogerian therapy in graduate school, and practiced classical psychoanalysis from 1947 to 1953. I soon became dissatisfied with psychoanalysis as a means of treatment because I appear to have been born with a "gene for efficiency" and I abandoned traditional analysis for the following reasons:

1. Psychoanalysis takes a considerable length of time and clients often remain in treatment literally for years.

2. One of the cardinal tenets of psychoanalysis is "with insight comes cure"; that is, once clients understand the nature of their conflicts, they will be able to overcome their difficulties. I found that even after clients had apparently gained insight into their problem, they continued to act in much the same disturbed manner (Ellis, 1962, 1994, 2001a, 2001b).

3. Although some clients improve under psychoanalytic treatment, few change the basic philosophy by which they make themselves and keep themselves disturbed.

In 1953, I began experimenting with cognitive, emotive, and behavioral techniques and began to be more active and directive in my therapy sessions. Rather than waiting for clients to gain insight into the nature of their disturbances, I would directly point out the inconsistencies in the client's reasoning and behaving. I also collaborated with them to take specific behavioral homework assignments. I noted (Ellis, 1962, p. 8) "Much to my surprise, this method actually started to produce not only quicker but apparently deeper and more lasting effects."

In January 1955, I called this new approach Rational Therapy (RT) and reported on it at the Annual Convention of the American Psychological Association in August 1956. However, the name Rational Therapy led some therapists to believe that the sole emphasis in this new form of therapy was on cognitions; that is, thoughts and beliefs. To the contrary, I have always maintained that cognitions, emotions, and behavior are interrelated. I wanted this new form of therapy to emphasize all three components and their interactions. The name was changed in 1961 to Rational-Emotive Therapy (RET) to avoid incorrect associations with the philosophical approach known as rationalism, which RET opposed. However, RET would have been more properly called Rational Emotive Behavioral Therapy (REBT), because it also encouraged clients to put their new beliefs into practice behaviorally and push themselves to act on them. Thus in 1993, I changed its name accordingly.

The Philosophical Underpinnings of REBT

Humans have a powerful predisposition or innate tendency to behave irrationally and self-defeatingly (Ellis, 1979). They have the tendency to avoid thinking things through, to procrastinate, to be overly suggestible, superstitious, and perfectionistic. But at the same time, they are healthy constructivists, with powerful innate tendencies to solve practical problems of living, to be creative, and to grow and develop (Ellis, 1994, 2001a, 2001b).

REBT theory states that humans also have a strong tendency to be influenced by their environment. This is particularly true during childhood, when family, peers, and culture have an enormous impact on their beliefs, emotions, and actions.

One of the primary tenets of REBT is that thoughts, feelings, and behaviors interact and significantly affect each other. Thinking affects, and in some ways creates, people's feelings and behaviors; their emotions have a very important effect on their thoughts and actions; and their actions distinctly influence their thoughts and feelings. If one of these processes is somehow altered, the other two are affected as well (Ellis, 1962, 1994, 1999, 2000; Ellis & Dryden, 1997; Ellis & MacLaren, 1998).

REBT acknowledges that virtually all humans are basically hedonistic because they are born with a strong tendency to avoid pain, remain alive, and seek happiness. However, it distinguishes between long-term and short-term hedonism in that it does not promote immediate and easy gratification at the expense of future gains.

A cardinal tenet of REBT is that all humans are fallible and have many limitations. REBT encourages people to fully accept themselves as children and adults who will now and forever make continual and numerous mistakes. It is important that they acknowledge their fallibility and still live happily by learning to unconditionally accept themselves despite their limitations.

The Twelve Irrational Beliefs

I originally described twelve major irrational beliefs that contribute to emotional disturbance (Ellis, 1958, 1962). These beliefs are listed below along with their rational alternatives.

1. *The Irrational Belief (IB) that you must—yes, must—have sincere love and approval all the time from all the people you find significant,* rather than the Rational Belief that you do not *have* to get what you want. By turning something that is desirable (e.g., money, peer support, approval) into something that is an absolute "necessity," you make yourself anxious and depressed when deprived of things you think you *must* have.

   Many adolescents place great importance on their standing with their peer group. This is a normal and natural developmental trend in adolescence. Their desire is taken to an unhealthy extreme when they think they "need" the approval of everyone whom they find significant. Seeking to acquire love and approval from everyone is not only unrealistic and unobtainable but will waste a good deal of time and energy (Wilde, 1995a). It is wiser for you to concentrate on accepting yourself with your positive and negative traits, rather than being overly concerned with the opinions of others. You cannot control what others think of you.

2. *The Irrational Belief that you must prove yourself to be thoroughly competent, adequate, and achieving; or that you must at least have unusual competence or talent at something important,* rather than the Rational Belief (RB) that *doing* is more important than *doing well.*

   It is understandable why you would *want* to do well. There are obvious advantages to success, such as higher grades or recognition for athletic achievements. It makes real sense to *want* to succeed. However, when you transfer your desire to perform well into a *need* or *necessity,* the potential for neurotic and self-defeating behavior increases dramatically. Success or failure takes on crucial importance. Achievement signifies that you are a "worthwhile human" and failure is the mark of your being a "worthless, unlovable" person.

   Only by *definition* do you make yourself worthwhile or worthless based on your achievements. Children's value as persons and their achievements are two entities that are often confused.

3. *The Irrational Belief that people who harm you or commit misdeeds rate as generally bad, wicked, or villainous individuals and that you should severely blame, damn, and punish them for their sins,* rather than the Rational Belief that all humans are fallible. REBT notes that it is irrational to extend a belief about your *behavior* to your self *as a whole.* Thus, your behavior can be "wrong" or "bad" but you, regardless of your misdeeds, are still a person who has both

positive and negative qualities. It is possible for you to behave in a reprehensible and irresponsible manner but still not be a *bad person.* REBT accepts the Christian philosophy that you accept the sinner but not necessarily his or her sins.

People have the privilege or right to act as they desire, even if we may not understand, appreciate, or agree with their behavior. Even when they behave in an immoral manner, they have the right to do so given that fact that they are human and possess some degree of choice or free will. They, alas, are prone to use their choice or free will inappropriately on many occasions.

4. *The Irrational Belief that life is awful, terrible, horrible, and catastrophic when things do not go the way you would like them to go,* rather than the self-helping, Rational Belief that many things are inconvenient but very few are catastrophic unless you *think* they are.

Words like "terrible," "awful," and "horrible" tend to carry with them the emotional meaning of "100% bad" or "worse than they must be." Practically nothing is so bad that you *cannot stand* it and cannot be happy *at all.* You can easily exaggerate an unfortunate event's occurrence into a "catastrophe" and thereby create needless anxiety and depression about it.

As I (JW) often point out to my clients, "How can you ever overcome a catastrophe? Let's try to keep thinking about this undesirable situation as a 'problem' and not create a 'catastrophe' about it. Problems are hard enough to overcome. We don't need 'catastrophes' too."

5. *The Irrational Belief that your emotional misery comes from external pressures and that you have little ability to control your feelings or rid yourself of depression and hostility,* rather than the Rational Belief that you are remarkably able to control how you think and behave. Because your thoughts influence and largely control your feelings, you can *choose* your emotional reaction to events. If you use it, you have distinct control over your reactions, thoughts, and emotions. By believing that others have the power to upset you, you give away your freedom and grant others gratuitous power over you.

Nearly any event that you can think of as "good" (e.g., buying a new house) can also produce other hassles (e.g., increased monthly mortgage payments and additional maintenance responsibilites.) Conversely, almost any event that you view as "bad" (e.g., a broken leg) you can also think of in a way to produce different advantages ("At least I can now get some reading done").

The idea that people have a great deal of control over their feelings and behaviors will not come as good news to everyone. Although this information is empowering, it can be frightening because it eliminates the scapegoats you have been blaming for your difficulties and places responsibility back in your own lap.

6. *The Irrational Belief that if something seems dangerous or fearsome, you must be obsessively occupied with and upset about it,* rather than the Rational Belief

that worrying about an event will not keep the event from occurring. It is healthy and appropriate for you to be "concerned" or "vigilant" about unfortunate happenings, because concern may help you take the corrective measures and be prepared for a potentially unpleasant event. To be *overly* concerned is a waste of time and energy, and limits your ability to enjoy many pleasures.

7. *The Irrational Belief that you will find it easier to avoid facing many of life's difficulties and self-responsibilities than to undertake some form of self-discipline,* rather than the Rational Belief that the so-called easy way out is often much harder in the long run (Ellis, 1962; Ellis & Harper, 1997). Shortcuts often lead to more difficulties in the future. Often the "long cut" turns out to be the best course of action.

   Avoiding a problem does not make the problem go away. Facing a difficult situation, rather than avoiding the inevitable, may be the best way to deal with it.

8. *The Irrational Belief that your past remains all-important and that because something once strongly influenced your life, it has to keep determining your feelings and behavior today,* rather than the Rational Belief that the past has an influence on the present but does not fully determine your present-day behavior. Your past does indeed give you reaction "tendencies" but you can become aware of them and work to make them less influential in your life.

   The past largely exists in memories and those memories are only impressions of the past as you once "experienced" it. Your memories are substantially influenced by your interpretations about and selective attention to past events. There is no such thing as purely "objective" history because each individual creates his or her own interpretation of the past. Realize that you have the ability to change, even though breaking old patterns can take considerable time and effort.

9. *The Irrational Belief that people and things must be better than they are; and that you have to experience life as awful and horrible if you do not quickly find good solutions to its hassles,* rather than the Rational Belief that there is no evidence that anything *has to be* different than it actually is. Believing otherwise leads you to feelings of rage and low frustration tolerance.

   Simply because some situations are painful or unpleasant does not mean that they *absolutely should not* be that way. *Everything is as it should be now* because all the prerequisites for a situation to exist have occurred. For example, *should* there be gun violence in America? That question can be answered by determining the prerequisites for gun violence. If the prerequisites have been met, then there should be gun violence.

   The prerequisites would seem to be:

   a. An ample supply of guns (more than 200 million guns would appear more than ample).

   b. People have the right and the ability to possess the guns.

c. A certain percentage of those people will be willing to fire those guns at other people.

d. People often have personal, social, economic, and other problems.

If these conditions are in effect, not only should there be many difficulties of living but some of these difficulties will most probably lead to gun violence.

Please do not think for one second that I (JW) am making light of America's heartbreaking problem with gun violence. I am merely trying to point out that *it is illogical and irrational to believe that things should not be exactly as they are at this time.* Once the prerequisites for an event exist, the event will likely occur. That may be quite unfortunate, but it still may be factual.

10. *The Irrational Belief that you can achieve happiness by inertia and inaction or by passively and uncommittedly "enjoying yourself,"* rather than the Rational Belief that you tend to be happy when you are creatively absorbed in some type of enjoyable and/or productive activity.

Individuals who passively participate in life rarely lead satisfying and rewarding existences. Finding a purpose or a goal to work toward usually gives you energy and vitality. An absorbing goal or rewarding activity can also be used to help you distract yourself from difficult situations.

Relaxing is certainly healthy but a life designed primarily to relax is usually relatively empty and lacking passion. The key in this equation, as it is in many things, is finding the right balance between work and play—too much or too little of either may be limiting.

11. *The Irrational Belief that you must have a high degree of certainty to feel comfortable,* rather than the Rational Belief that very few certainties, if any, exist in the universe. Even without perfect order and certainty you can still be relatively happy most of the time.

Many people are capable of tolerating uncertainty and accepting that they have only a high degree of probability, but no certainty, that they will fulfill their desires. As stated earlier, no one *has to* have what he or she wants. Certainty may be desirable in some instances, but this does not mean that it absolutely must exist. The universe is not run according to our desires.

12. *The Irrational Belief that you can give yourself a global rating as a human and that your general self-worth and self-acceptance depend on the goodness of your performance and degree to which people approve of you,* rather than the self-helping and Rational Belief that you and other people are too complex to be given a global rating for your and their actions. You cannot be given a general grade or a rating for a few of your behaviors.

All humans have many positive and negative traits. The "good" and "bad" actions do not balance each other out. As Alfred Korzybski (1933–1990) stated, you never *are* what you do, because you do thousands of things—good, bad, and indifferent—in your lifetime, and it is never known what you will do in the future. With this in mind, it is best to simply accept yourself as inherently worthwhile because your once-for-all-time "worth" is uncalculatable (Ellis, 1962, 1994, 2000, 2001b; Ellis & Harper, 1997).

It is best to refuse to rate or evaluate your infinitely complex *self, personality,* or *being* at all but merely to rate the helpful things you do for yourself and others as "good" and your unhelpful and unhealthy thoughts, feelings, and behaviors as "bad." Again, global ratings of your *essence* or *youness* are misleading and, as Korzybski said, tend to make you "unsane," or neurotic but not insane.

Techniques of Rational Emotive Behavior Therapy

REBT therapists typically employ a large variety of cognitive, affective, and behavioral techniques in the course of therapy. These techniques are used on practical as well as theoretical grounds, given the REBT premise that thoughts, feelings, and behaviors function interactively.

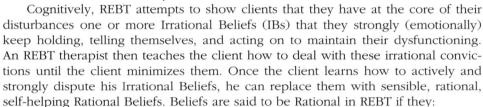

Cognitively, REBT attempts to show clients that they have at the core of their disturbances one or more Irrational Beliefs (IBs) that they strongly (emotionally) keep holding, telling themselves, and acting on to maintain their dysfunctioning. An REBT therapist then teaches the client how to deal with these irrational convictions until the client minimizes them. Once the client learns how to actively and strongly dispute his Irrational Beliefs, he can replace them with sensible, rational, self-helping Rational Beliefs. Beliefs are said to be Rational in REBT if they:

1. Are accurate and factual;
2. Can be supported by evidence or realistic proof;
3. Are logical;
4. Are not absolutistic commands or demands;
5. Are desires, wishes, hopes, and preferences;
6. Produce healthy negative emotions, such as sadness, irritation, and concern and nondysfunctional behaviors when unfortunate events occur; and
7. Help people to reach their desired individual and social goals.

Beliefs are said to be Irrational if they:

1. Are inaccurate or contradicted by facts;
2. Lead to false deductions;
3. Consist of overgeneralizations;
4. Are absolutistic commands, shoulds, musts, and needs;
5. Lead to disturbed emotions such as depression, rage, and anxiety and to dysfunctional behaviors, such as compulsions or avoidances; and
6. Hinder people from reaching their goals (Walen, DiGiuseppe, & Wessler, 1992).

An REBT therapist will often ask clients to explain what they are telling themselves about a troubling event. When clients have identified the Beliefs they have about this event, the therapist asks for proof that the Belief is accurate, self-helping, and rational. This process resembles a discussion in which clients are asked to weigh the evidence that shows whether the Beliefs will help or hinder them. If the Beliefs seem to be dysfunctional or destructive, the clients are assisted in changing them to self-helping Rational Beliefs.

For example, clients may believe, "Life has to be fair." Using REBT disputing, this Belief is shown to be self-defeating in that life obviously *does not have to be* fair, although that is *preferable;* and this idea will therefore often lead to rage and depression. Once the client understands and agrees with this notion, the Belief can be changed to a rational philosophy such as "I would like it if life were totally fair, but because I would *prefer* life to be fair does not mean it *has to* be that way; too bad that it often isn't."

Emotively, REBT therapists use several techniques, such as fully accepting their clients no matter how unhealthy and dysfunctional their behavior. A technique known as Rational Emotive Imagery is often used during the course of which clients are encouraged to imagine a very unfortunate situation and let themselves feel anxious, depressed, or enraged. While imagining this scenario, clients are encouraged to change their irrational thinking regarding the event and thereby feel the healthy negative emotions of sorrow, regret, and frustration. Therapists also use techniques such as shame-attacking exercises in which clients are encouraged to perform "shameful" or embarrassing acts but encouraged to try not to feel embarrassed, ashamed, or self-downing. The use of humor to clarify and illustrate important points to a client is also frequently employed (Ellis, 1999, 2000, 2001a, 2001b; Ellis & Dryden, 1997; Ellis & MacLaren, 1998).

Behaviorally, REBT therapists use nearly all standard behavioral techniques such as operant conditioning, self-reinforcement, and relaxation training. They especially employ in vivo desensitization or exposure to help clients actively face their phobias and fears. For example, if clients are afraid of riding elevators, they are encouraged to do just that as often as possible until they no longer experience anxiety at the thought of using them.

INTERACTIVE NATURE OF TECHNIQUES OF RATIONAL EMOTIVE THERAPY

Typically, cognitive, emotive, and behavioral techniques are used in conjunction with one another and even simultaneously. In the previously mentioned example, a client may be asked to ride the elevator while emotionally and forcefully telling himself a rational coping statement such as, "There is no proof that riding in an elevator is terrible, awful, and catastrophic. I am in control of my anxiety if I stop dreaming up horrors that will ensue if I keep using elevators."

The REBT approach typically uses a model of coping with problems called the ABCs. In this model, *A* is known as the Activating Event or Adversity. In other words, *A* is an Activating Event that clients believe is upsetting them. At *C* (Consequence), they experience an emotional reaction such as anger, guilt, or depression. Typically, the client attributes the emotional reaction at C to the Adversity at point A. The therapist's task is to bring to the client's awareness that it is not only the event at point A that is causing his emotional reaction at point C. The causes of his disturbed feelings are A (Adversity) *plus* B (his Belief *about A*), thus $A + B = C$. For example, if a client is depressed (at point C) about receiving a failing mark on a test (at point A), the failing mark is not directly the cause of the depression. According to REBT theory, the client's dysfunctional emotion is brought about by his failure *plus* his irrational belief at B. In this scenario, the client might hold the Irrational Belief "I *must not* fail at this test and, if I do, I am an *inadequate person* for failing." Such a belief would be disputed at point D (Disputing) to help the client realize that his belief is self-defeating, inaccurate, and irrational. Factually and logically, receiving a failing mark is certainly undesirable but there is no reason why the client absolutely *must* pass the test, and failing it is *unfortunate* but hardly makes him an *inadequate person*. The client's Irrational Belief or self-statement is an example of overgeneralization or "awfulizing," which is irrational and self-defeating.

EMPIRICAL EVIDENCE SUPPORTING REBT INTERVENTIONS WITH CHILDREN AND ADOLESCENTS

Although it is beyond the scope of this book to present detailed and exhaustive findings regarding the efficacy of REBT with children and adolescents, it is hoped that providing an overview of the data can help the reader to analyze and draw his or her own conclusions from the original sources of empirical research showing the results of REBT with school-aged populations. The studies cited below are some examples of the wide range of clinical applications of REBT with children and ado-lescents.

REBT has been found to be successful with youngsters in the following studies: (1) to reduce anxiety (Brody, 1974; Cangelosi, Gressard, & Mines, 1980; DiGiuseppe & Kassinove, 1976; Knaus & Bokor, 1975; Knaus & McKeever, 1977; Meyer, 1981; Miller & Kassinove, 1978; Omizo, Lo, & Williams, 1986; Von Pohl, 1982; Warren, Deffenbacher, & Brading, 1976); (2) to increase frustration tolerance (Brody, 1974); (3) to reduce impulsivity (Meichenbaum & Goodman, 1971); (4) to improve academic performance (Block, 1978; Cangelosi, Gressard, & Mines, 1980), (5) to reduce depression (Wilde, 1994); and (6) to improve self-concept and coping capabilities (DeVoge, 1974; DiGiuseppe, 1975; DiGiuseppe & Kassinove, 1976; Ellis, 1979; Katz, 1974; Maultsby, Knipping, & Carpenter, 1974; Omizo, Lo, & Williams, 1986; Wasserman & Vogrin, 1979). In addition, several studies have examined REBT and shown its effectiveness in improving rational thinking in students: DiGiuseppe & Kassinove, 1976; Harris, 1976; Knaus & Bokor, 1975; Lipsky, Kassinove, &

Carpenter, 1980; Miller & Kassinove, 1978; Ribowitz, 1979; Ritchie, 1978; Voelm, 1983; Wasserman & Vogrin, 1979; and Wilde, 1994.

Several books have been written summarizing the use of REBT with children and adolescents, including those by Bernard (2001), Bernard and Joyce (1984), Ellis and Bernard (1983), Wilde (1995b), and Vernon (1989, 1999).

Goals of Rational Emotive Behavior Therapy

1. To make clients more aware of their self-talk and internal dialogue and particularly of their self-defeating Beliefs, so that they will be able to think more rationally, clearly, logically and helpfully.

2. To teach clients to evaluate their thinking, feeling, and behavior in order to experience more healthy emotions and fewer dysfunctions.

3. To teach clients the skills to use rational emotive behavioral principles so they will act more functionally and be better able to achieve their goals in life (Wilde, 1992).

The following verbatim cases in this book are designed to give readers an "inside look" into the therapeutic process of REBT. Often the finest and most detailed descriptions of the techniques and interventions used in counseling sessions still leave sizable gaps as to what actually happens in therapy.

One of the best ways to use REBT techniques is by "sitting in" on the verbatim transcripts of sessions with experienced therapists, "listening" to their choice of words, questions, and their actions. Reading these transcripts is also beneficial for young or inexperienced therapists to help them see that there are many different ways of practicing REBT. As you examine the following verbatim descriptions of REBT sessions with children, try to pay particular attention to the similarities and differences in the styles of the various therapists who have submitted these cases. It is hoped that through exposure to this diversity of styles, you will be able to learn the interventions that will complement your individual approaches to working with children. It is our sincere hope that you learn considerably about the cognitive, emotional, and behavioral problems of youngsters that are ably dealt with by the REBT practitioners in this book.

References

Bernard, M. E. (2001). *Program achieve* (2nd ed.). Laguna Beach, CA: You Can Do It! Education.

Bernard, M. E., & Joyce, M. R. (1984). *Rational-emotive therapy with children and adolescents*. New York: Wiley.

Block, J. (1978). Effects of rational-emotive mental health program on poorly achieving, disruptive high school students. *Journal of Counseling Psychology, 25,* 61–65.

Brody, M. (1974). *The effects of rational-emotive affective education on anxiety, self-esteem, and frustration tolerance*. Unpublished doctoral dissertation, Temple University, Philadelphia.

Cangelosi, A., Gressard, C., & Mines, R. (1980). The effects of rational thinking groups on self-concepts in adolescents. *The School Counselor, 14,* 357–361.

DeVoge, C. (1974). A behavioral approach to RET with children. *Rational Living, 9,* 23–26.

DiGiuseppe, R. (1975). *A developmental study on the efficacy of rational-emotive education.* Unpublished doctoral dissertation, New York: Hofstra University.

DiGiuseppe, R., & Kassinove, H. (1976). Effects of a rational-emotive school mental health program in children's emotional adjustment. *Journal of Community Psychology, 4,* 382–387.

Ellis, A. (1958). Rational psychotherapy. *Journal of General Psychology,* 59, 35–49.

Ellis, A. (1962). *Reason and emotion in psychotherapy.* Secaucus, NJ: Citadel.

Ellis, A. (1979). The theory of rational-emotive therapy. In A. Ellis & J. Whiteley (Eds.), *Theoretical and empirical foundations of rational-emotive therapy.* (pp. 9–26). Monterey, CA: Brooks/Cole.

Ellis, A. (1994). *Reason and emotion in psychotherapy* (rev. ed.). New York: Kensington.

Ellis, A. (1999). *How to be happy and remarkably less disturbable.* Atascadero, CA: Impact.

Ellis, A. (2000). *How to control your anxiety before it controls you.* New York: Citadel.

Ellis, A. (2001a). *Feeling better, getting better, staying better.* Atascadero, CA: Impact.

Ellis, A. (2001b). *Overcoming destructive thoughts, feelings, and behaviors.* Amherst, NY: Prometheus Books.

Ellis, A., & Bernard, M. E. (Eds.) (1983). *Rational-emotive therapy approaches to the problems of childhood.* New York: Plenum.

Ellis, A., & Dryden, W. (1997). *The practice of rational-emotive behavior therapy.* New York: Springer.

Ellis, A., & MacLaren, C. (1998). *Rational-emotive behavior therapy: A therapist's guide.* Atascadero, CA: Impact.

Ellis, A., & Harper, R. (1997). *A guide to rational living.* North Hollywood, CA: Wilshire.

Epictetus (1840). *The works of Epictetus.* Boston: Little, Brown.

Harris, S. (1976). Rational-emotive education and the human development program: A guidance study. *Elementary School Guidance and Counseling, 10,* 113–122.

Katz, S. (1974). *The effect of emotional education on locus of control and self-concept.* Unpublished doctoral dissertation, New York: Hofstra University.

Knaus, W., & Bokor, S. (1975). The effects of rational-emotive education on anxiety and self-concept. *Rational Living, 10,* 7–10.

Knaus, W., & McKeever, C. (1977). Rational-emotive education on anxiety and self-concept. *Rational Living, 12,* 7–10.

Korzybski, A. (1900/1933). *Science and sanity.* Concord, CA: International Society of General Semantics.

Lipsky, M., Kassinove, H, & Miller, N. (1980). Effects of rational-emotive therapy, rational role reversal and rational-emotive imagery on the emotional adjustment of community mental health center patients. *Journal of Consulting and Clinical Psychology, 48,* 366–374.

Maultsby, M., Knipping, P., & Carpenter, L. (1974). Teaching self-help in the classroom with rational self-counseling. *Journal of School Health, 44,* 445–448.

Meichenbaum, D., & Goodman, J. (1971). Training impulsive children to talk to themselves. *Journal of Abnormal Psychology, 77,* 115–126.

Meyer, D. (1981). *Effects of rational-emotive therapy upon anxiety and self-esteem of learning disabled children.* Ann Arbor: University of Michigan.

Miller, N., & Kassinove, H. (1978). Effects of behavioral rehearsal, written homework, and level of intelligence on the efficacy of rational-emotive education in elementary school children. *Journal of Community Psychology, 6,* 366–373.

Omizo, M., Lo, F., & William, R. (1986). Rational-emotive education, self-concept, and locus of control among learning disabled students. *Journal of Humanistic Education and Development, 25,* 59–69.

Ribowitz, A. (1979). *Effects of "ABC" homework sheets, initial level of adjustment, and duration of treatment on the efficacy of rational-emotive education in elementary school children.* Unpublished doctoral dissertation, Hofstra University, New York.

Ritchie, B. (1978). *The effects of rational-emotive education on irrational beliefs, assertiveness, and/or locus of control in fifth grade students.* Unpublished doctoral dissertation, Virginia Polytechnic University, Blacksburg, VA.

Voelm, C. (1983). *The efficacy of teaching rational-emotive education to acting-out and socially withdrawn adolescents.* Unpublished doctoral dissertation, California School of Professional Psychology, Los Angeles.

Vernon, A. (1989). *Thinking, feeling, behaving: An emotional education curriculum for children, grades 1–6.* Champaign, IL: Research.

Vernon, A. (1999). *The passport program.* Champaign, IL: Research.

Von Pohl, R. (1982). *A study to assess the effects of rational-emotive therapy with a selected group of emotionally disturbed children in day and residential treatment.* Unpublished doctoral dissertation, University of Alabama, Birmingham.

Walen, S., DiGiuseppe, R., & Wessler, R. (1992). *A practitioner's guide to rational-emotive therapy.* New York: Oxford University Press.

Wasserman, T., & Vogrin, D. (1979). Relationship of endorsement of rational beliefs, age, months treatment and intelligence to overt behavior of emotionally disturbed children. *Psychological Reports, 44,* 911–917.

Warren, R., Deffenbacher, J., & Brading, P. (1976). Rational-emotive therapy and the reduction of test anxiety in elementary school students. *Rational Living, 11,* 28–29.

Wilde, J. (1992). *Rational counseling with school aged populations: A practical guide.* Muncie, IN: Accelerated Development.

Wilde, J. (1994). The effects of the *Let's get rational* board game on rational thinking, depression, and self-acceptance in adolescents. *The Journal of Rational-Emotive & Cognitive-Behavior Therapy, 12,* 189–196.

Wilde, J. (1995a). *Anger management in schools: Alternatives to student violence.* Lancaster, PA: Technomic Publishing.

Wilde, J. (1995b). *Treating anger, anxiety and depression in children and adolescents: A cognitive behavioral approach.* Philadelphia: Taylor & Francis.

A 17-Year-Old Boy With School Difficulties and Anger Problems

Therapist: Howard Young

It is difficult to provide more detail in the way of an introduction to this case because the therapist, Howard Young, passed away several years ago. The authors would like to thank Michele Young for permission to use this case in the book.

This interview was conducted with "Dave," a 17-year-old boy, who was referred by his parents. The primary presenting problem was Dave's truancy, but there were also concerns about his temper, which caused him to get into trouble.

THERAPIST: What brings you to see a counselor?

CLIENT: (sarcastically) My car!

T: Clever! You mean you have a car problem? If so, you're in the wrong place. You need a mechanic, not a head shrinker. I help people with mental and emotional problems.

C: (even more sarcastically) Then I don't belong here, because I'm not mental. I'm not crazy.

T: You certainly don't seem crazy to me. Who told you to come here for help?

C: My a—— parents!

T: What reason did they give you for sending you to a counselor?

C: I don't know. Why don't you ask them?

T: I can't. They're not here now. But I think I know what your problem is.

C: (very defiantly) What?

T: You've got problem parents. You've got parents that think they know everything. They plan your life for you, and you don't like it; they figure there's something wrong with you, not them!

C: You're godda—— right! My parents are all f—— up! They're all over my case.

T: Then you're in the right place.

C: What do you mean?

T: I specialize in problem parents. I can help you learn to manage your parents better.

C: I don't need your help!

T: Sure you do! You're getting nowhere doing things your way. In fact, that's what got you here, isn't it? Do you like being here?

[*JW: Just in case some of you might not recognize genius while you're reading it, please look over the last few exchanges carefully. Howard Young was very adept at disarming defiant youths and this paradoxical technique is something I highly recommend.*]

C: No!

T: I'll bet coming here isn't the only hassle you've had to endure because of your parents.

C: Yeah. They won't allow me to drive the car, and no one's allowed to come over to the house.

T: The more you fight them the worse it gets. And you're telling me you don't need help with your parents?

C: What kind of help?

T: First, help in controlling your temper. I've talked to you just a little while, but it seems your temper is a problem. Second, I can show you how to talk to your parents so you don't always end up in trouble.

C: Yeah, I got a temper. My friends are all afraid of me when I get mad. They think I'm crazy.

T: Okay, then, let's start with your temper. Give me an example of the last time you got really mad and lost your cool.

C: That's easy. An hour ago, when they told me I had to see you.

T: Okay, now me let ask you this: What do you think made you mad?

C: I told you: My parents making me see you.

T: I'd like you to consider another possibility: Maybe you're the one who made you feel angry.

C: Me? I didn't make myself come in here. They did!

T: No, no, Dave. I'm suggesting it's your attitude about your parents' making you come in that did the damage and got you upset. Sure, they told you what to do, but it was your brain that turned a pain in the ass into a major crime! Here, let me show you what I mean. Take this. (Howard Young hands the client a rubber hammer). Now, suppose you were to hit yourself over the head with it. Whose fault would it be? Whom would you blame?

C: Me!

T: Even if I was the one who gave the hammer to you?

C: You just handed it to me. It would be my fault if I hit myself over the head with it.

T: Dave, it's the same with your parents' making you come here. (Dave looks inquisitive.) They hand you crap and you hit yourself over the head with it. They tell you what to do, and you make a big deal, a major crime out of it. (Dave nods attentively.) So it's not what they do, but what you do in your mind that's causing your anger. You're blaming your parents for something you're doing to yourself. They keep handing you the hammer, and you keep hitting yourself over the head with it. You put all your energy into blaming them instead of working on a way to stop giving yourself a hard time.

[JW: More "gold" from Howard Young.]

C: You mean my parents have nothing to do with it? I make it all up?

T: That's a good question, Dave, because that's not what I mean. Your parents contribute—they dish it out. But it's the way you take it, the way you blow it up in your mind, that's the real cause of your anger. Your parents play a part—they're not innocent bystanders—but you're the one that's mentally making a big deal out of it. (A pause while Dave considers what has been said.)

C: It makes sense I guess. I never thought about it that way.

T: Would you like to learn what kind of thinking makes you angry? (Dave shrugs his shoulders in resigned agreement.) Okay, let's use an illustration. I'm not an artist, but maybe this cartoon will help you understand. (Howard Young draws a face that looks angry and puts a thought bubble next to it. The bubble is left blank.) You notice I left the idea part blank, because I want you to help me fill it in. What went through your mind right after your parents told you that you had to come in and see me?

C: Oh s——! Here we go again! I'm fed up with all this s——! Enough is enough! (Howard Young writes in the thought bubble "I can't stand it anymore!")

T: Anything else?

C: Who do they think they are? Why can't they get off my back? They've f—— up my life! (Howard Young writes "They've got no right telling me what to do!")

T: Is this it? Is this what went through your mind when your parents told you that you had to see me?

C: That's what I was trying to say. Especially that last one. I think that all the time.

T: These two ideas not only get *you* angry, but they probably would get anyone just as upset. In fact, these are two of the nuttiest ideas people think. Would you like to learn how to change these ideas, feel less angry, stop blaming your parents, and get a grip on your temper? Or maybe you want to keep having temper tantrums.

C: No, the anger gets me into trouble. I got kicked out of school one time because of a stupid fight.

T: Okay. Here's how we do it. First, we see if the ideas make any sense or if they're just bulls——. We'll tackle that "I can't stand it anymore" idea. Do you really believe that you can't stand it when your parents tell you what to do and try to run your life?

C: It seems as though I can't, as though it's too much, sometimes it's . . .

T: It's what you make of it. "It" doesn't have any power over you at all. For example, is your parents' interference in your life difficult to handle or is it impossible to handle? Which is it? Difficult or impossible?

C: Well, difficult, I guess.

T: Why isn't it impossible? (A blank look crosses Dave's face) If it were impossible to put up with your parents, you would've been killed off by now, but you're still alive. In other words, no matter how much of a pain in the ass your parents give you, you've survived, haven't you?

C: Yeah.

T: Suppose that the next time your parents tell you to do something stupid, such as coming to see me, you tell yourself, "Here we go again. Sure, it's the same old bulls—— but it won't kill me. I can stand it, even though I don't like it." How do you think you'd feel?

C: If I could feel that? A lot less angry.

T: Okay, let's look at the other anger-producing idea. (Howard Young points to the cartoon and to "They've got no right telling me what to do.")

C: Well, they don't have a right. I've got my rights . . .

T: Okay, wait a minute. Let me agree with you on one thing. It's wrong for your parents to order you around and tell you what to do. Your parents are wrong, okay?

C: You're godda—— right!

T: Are your parents human?

C: Yeah.

T: Do humans make mistakes?

C: Yeah.

T: Do your parents have the right to make a mistake, like bossing you around?

C: Not when it comes to me. They ought to know . . .

T: Are your parents human? Do human make mistakes? Isn't it human nature to do wrong things?

C: Yeah.

T: Do your parents have a right to be wrong? Even when they're bossing you around and trying to run your life?

C: Yeah, I guess so, when you put it that way.

T: Suppose the next time they tell you what to do, the next time they make you do something you don't like, you say to yourself, "It's wrong, but they have the right to be wrong. After all they're f——— up humans like everyone else!" How angry do you think you'd feel if you thought things out like that?

C: If I could think that way, it wouldn't bother me so much.

[*AE: As Jerry Wilde notes, Howard Young was something of a genius in talking to difficult children and adolescents, most of whom came from the Bible Belt in West Virginia. In this session, he is not thrown by the rough language of his adolescent client but he humorously and directly shows him one of the many ABCs of REBT: Namely that the client* chooses *to upset himself at* C *(his angry consequences) by irrationally Believing (B)* "They shouldn't *bother me so much! I can't stand it!" In just a few minutes, Howard Young helps the client see that* he and his Beliefs (B), *rather than his restricting parents (A), make him mad (C). He also proposes to the client the Rational Belief, "My parents may be wrong but they are fallible people who have the right to be wrong!" Succinctly and beautifully done—in the usual Howard Young style!*]

CASE
2

A 10-Year-Old Boy
With Peer Problems

Therapist: Terry London

This case involves a 10-year-old boy who was referred by a school social worker because of his difficulty with verbal taunting from the other children in his classes. He would either become very angry and fight or start to cry and withdraw completely from his peers. He was a bright boy who seemed to be normal in physical appearance and had reasonably good social skills. It seems that the original conflict started when he transferred to the school the previous year because his family had moved. A peer group he wanted to enter had some aggressive leaders who had started to go after him with name calling and hostile put-downs. The cycle was set. When they got the reinforcement they were seeking, namely seeing him upset and fighting, they increased the frequency and intensity of their verbal arrows, and he found it more and more difficult not to upset himself. The excerpts from this case will illustrate how to use an REBT approach when working with a child.

When using REBT with children, the following guidelines, I believe, are important and govern my decisions in therapy.

1. Actively teach the relationship between thinking and emotions.
2. De-emphasize the Disputing (*D*) step and instead use role-plays, modeling, and story-telling techniques to teach rational coping statements.
3. Use visual aids, cartoons, tape-recordings, and hands-on experiences.

4. Get the child to practice and rehearse his or her new skills by thinking out loud during role-plays and simulations.

5. Use language and concepts that are at the cognitive level of the child.

This client's specific Irrational Beliefs were:

1. "It hurts me when they call me names."
2. "I can't stand it when they treat me unfairly."
3. "I'm bad or no good when they don't like me."

He also had difficulty in deciding what would be the most effective way to cope with his tormentors. He vacillated from firm assertion to fighting, and then finally gave up and retreated. This practical problem was also addressed in the therapy sessions.

FIRST SESSION

THERAPIST: Hi, that's sure a cool shirt you got on.

CLIENT: Thanks.

T: Did mom tell you my name?

C: Yeah.

T: What is it?

C: Terry.

T: That's right. And yours is S., right?

C: Right.

T: S., have you ever talked to a person like me before? I mean a counselor or psychologist.

C: Well, kinda—at school, I guess she's a social worker.

T: That's right, she's a social worker. I think Mrs. A. is a real nice lady. Do you like her, too?

C: Yeah, she's my friend.

T: Good, we have a mutual buddy. Now when I work with guys like you, I see myself as kind of a coach. I don't coach them in baseball or basketball, but I coach them in dealing with the rough spots in their life. Do you know what a rough spot is?

C: Hum, not really.

T: I use the word rough spot to mean anything that you find unfair, or helps to get you upset, or you find real difficult. Make sense?

C: (Nods) Yeah.

T: Like if I go to use my car and it has a flat tire, that's a rough spot. Or if someone yells at me, that's a rough spot, too. See?

C: (Nods) Yeah.

T: Now, I have been told, S., by your mother and Mrs. A., that you have some rough spots at school. Is that true?

C: Yeah, that's true.

T: I know it's not much fun to talk about rough spots, S., but it's the only way we can shrink them and make them smoother so you can deal with them. What's your rough spot?

C: The other kids call me names and make fun of me!

T: Wow! That's a big rough spot to deal with. When they call you those names, how do you feel?

C: Mad! I want to get them.

T: Could it be that you also feel hurt and bad inside?

C: Yeah, that too, sometimes.

T: Do you agree that when you get real upset, the rough spot gets even bigger and rougher to deal with?

C: Yeah.

At this point, I take out of my desk a large, thick, big balloon that has "rough spot" written on it. This is one of my favorite visual aids to work on decreasing the intensity of the emotional response. Children find the concept of less intensity too abstract. This is concrete and, of course, visual.

T: Now, let's say, S., that this balloon is your rough spot and I'm going to start blowing it up until it matches how big your rough spot is—Okay? You tell me when to stop.

C: Okay.

T: Big enough yet?

C: Nah.

T: What do you think?

C: Maybe a little bigger.

T: Wow! It sure is a big rough spot! Any bigger and it will explode!

C: (laughs) That would be awesome to see it bust!

T: Oh, really.

C: Yeah!

T: Now, S., if this is how big your rough spot is, I can understand why you're having problems. Even Superman would have difficulties! Do you agree that we would have to shrink this rough spot down in size in order to deal with it?

C: (nods) Yeah.

T: Well, I can coach you, and together we can learn how to smooth it out and shrink it down, so you can manage it a lot better. Interested?

C: (nods) Sure!

T: Before we even get into how to shrink it down, first let's see how small it would have to be so you could deal with it, Okay?

C: (nods) Okay.

T: (start to let the air out slowly) Small enough?

C: (shakes head) No.

T: Well, small enough yet?

C: Hum—no.

T: Pretty small now, I think you could handle it now?

C: Sure!

Obviously, the size of the balloon is an arbitrary reference point, but it's useful in that the child has a visual referent to work towards. The rest of the session was spent building rapport with S. I reinforced the idea of shrinking the rough spot together next time we met. He left in an upbeat mood.

SECOND SESSION

T: Hey, S., how are you doing?

C: Okay.

T: Good. Any rough spots since I last saw you?

C: Nope, not really.

T: That's good. Remember I said we are going to work together on learning how to shrink rough spots, right?

C: Right.

T: Okay. To learn how to become good at shrinking those rough spots down in our lives, we have to get good at two things. First, learning how to build emotional muscle or how to stay cool and not get too upset over the rough spot. Second, making up a plan of attack to deal with it. Make sense?

C: (nods) Yeah.

T: The first real important idea that we have to understand in order to keep our cool is that our feelings mainly come from the way we think about things or situations. The way we think is the way we feel. The way we think is the way we feel. Can you say that out loud? (I also always point to my head and my belly when I go over this.)

C: The way we think is the way we feel.

T: Oh, very good. Remember to point to your head. The way we think is the way we feel (point to belly). Your turn.

C: The way we think (points to his head) is the way we feel (points to his belly).

T: Great!—Now, S., let me give you an example of this thinking rule. Two boys are walking down the street when they see a giant dog walking towards them. The first boy thinks (point to my head), "Oh boy, I love big dogs. He reminds me of my Grandpa's dog. I hope he won't run away and will play with us." Now, S. (pointing to my belly), how do you think he feels?

C: Oh, he's happy.

T: Right. Now the second boy sees the dog and starts to think (point to my head). "Oh no—the last time I saw a dog, he tried to bite me, and this dog's a big one. If he's mean he could really hurt me." Now, S., how do you think the second boy (pointing to my belly) feels?

C: Scared!

T: Right again. So do you see that our feelings come from our thoughts or how we self-talk about stuff in our life.

C: Yeah.

T: Okay. So, if we want to not be so upset over something in our life, like a rough spot, the best way to change the feelings is to change the. . . . (I point to my head.)

C: The thinking.

T: You got it! You got it! Very good!

This session introduced the relationship between cognition and emotion in a simple concrete fashion. The rest of the session was spent going over many different illustrations of this principle. I gave S. a written homework assignment where he had to write down what a person was feeling based on what appeared in thought bubbles.

SESSION THREE

T: S., now that you really understand that you control your feelings by the way you think about a situation, it's time we talked about hot thoughts and cool thoughts. Okay?

C: (nods) Okay.

T: A hot thought is a thought that when we think it, it makes us upset and makes it harder to deal with a rough spot. A cool thought is a thought that keeps us pretty calm and allows us to deal with a rough spot better. Make sense?

C: (nods) Yeah.

T: Okay. Here's the rough spot. My sister took my bike without asking me if it was Okay. When I find out, I start to think, "How dare she!—She can't do this!—It drives me crazy!—I can't stand this!" Are they hot or cool thoughts?

C: Hot, hot.

T: You got it! And how big would my rough spot be?

C: Real big.

T: Right! Bigger than it has to be. Now, if I was thinking this, "Stop, take a deep breath. Relax—Good for me, I'm in control—I don't like what she did, but I can deal with it. It's not the end of the world, just unpleasant." Are these hot thoughts or cool thoughts?

C: Cool thoughts!

T: Right!—And how big would my rough spot be?

C: A lot smaller.

T: You got it!

The rest of this session was spent discussing what cool thoughts he could use regarding his situation of name calling and being teased. The following excerpt taken from this session is a story I often use to help children understand how their emotional response can reinforce exactly the behavior that they dislike being directed toward them.

T: People can name call or tease for a lot of different reasons, but one of the major reasons people keep doing it is because they enjoy getting you to bite their hook.

C: What does that mean?

T: Have you ever gone fishing?

C: A lot of times with my dad and grandpa.

T: All right, so we get our fishing gear, take our boat out to the middle of the lake, bait our hooks, throw them into the water, and then the fish really start biting our hooks. Do we want to fish more or less?

C: Oh, a lot more, that's when it's fun!

T: Right! Now, if we did exactly the same thing, get our gear, row out to the middle of the lake, bait our hooks, throw them into the water, and then nothing at all, not even a nibble all day long. Do we want to fish more or less?

C: Less, that's no fun.

T: Now, can you see when the kids at school go fishing for you with their verbal bait and hooks and you bite the hook, they want to . . . ?

C: Oh, I see, they want to fish more.

T: Right! So you have to learn how not to bite their hooks!

C: Oh, yeah!

FIFTH SESSION

In the next two sessions, we continued to practice a set of cool thoughts that would lead to a much more healthy emotional and behavioral response. S. did a great job of practicing his self-instructions outside our therapy sessions. The cool thoughts that he decided on were:

STOP!

1. Take a deep breath. Relax.
2. I don't like what they say, but I can deal with it.
3. Good for me, I'm not biting the bait. I'm staying cool.
4. Just walk away now and stay calm.

His homework consisted of practicing thinking his cool thoughts out loud at least 10 minutes per day with his parents, listening to himself on a tape recorder afterwards, and deciding how strong and believable he sounded.

T: Boy, you sound great on this tape from last week! Do you think you really feel your cool thoughts deep down so you could deal with the rough spot of being teased and called names?

C: (with pride) I have already!

T: You have? Tell me about it.

C: Well, do you remember about this guy named Ray I told you about?

T: I do. He's kind of a bully and a lot of time gives you a lot of crap.

C: He was trying to get me to fight with him at lunch and I just kept thinking my cool thoughts and he finally just let me alone.

T: Wow, that's terrific! How do you feel about not biting the hook?

C: Cool.

T: Yes!—Now, I think you're ready for a little rough spot role-playing with me. I'm going to pretend to be the worst bully in the world. Don't worry, I won't slug you, just be ready to stay cool because I'm going to be real mean and nasty to you. So, S., what I want you to do is think your cool thoughts out loud along with any other way of thinking so you won't upset yourself, and keep the rough spot small. Okay—Ready?

C: Ready.

When doing this type of role-playing, it is vital that the therapist be quite evocative, powerful, and "emotionally real" in the role of aggressor for two reasons:

1. If the child cannot control his emotional response in a safe role-play, it is highly unlikely he will in the real situation.
2. The emotional intensity of the role-play must come close to the level of arousal that would take place in the real situation, otherwise the skills will not transfer adequately.

All of this done by the therapist in a loud, nasty, aggressive, somewhat vicious way.

T: You faggot!

C: I don't like what he says, but I can deal with it.

T: You're so stupid and wimpy!

C: I'm not going to bite the hook.

T: You know everyone hates you!

C: Stop. Take a deep breath. Relax.

T: Oh, pretending you don't care.

C: Stay cool. Don't bite the hook.

T: Baby! Baby! Baby!

C: Just because he says so does not make it true. Stay cool.

T: You're the worst kid in the whole school when it comes to sports. Nobody wants you on their team.

C: Good for me, I'm not biting the bait. I'm staying cool!

T: Why don't you say something, fool?

C: Just walk away now and stay calm.

T: (calmly now) End of role-play. You did great. It seemed like you never upset yourself at all. I can be pretty mean, can't I?

C: You sure can!

T: But you stayed cool and even came up with a new cool thought. That was excellent. How do you feel about how you handled it?

C: Real good!

POSTSCRIPT

This child did exceptionally well in a very short period of time. He enjoyed his new "thinking skill" of cool thoughts and had a sense of pride about controlling his behavior. He even did a presentation to his class on how to deal with rough spots and self-talking. The total number of sessions totaled 17, with 2-week intervals after the first 11 sessions. The sessions consisted of rehearsal of coping statements, role-plays, and general problem-solving. His all-time favorite cool thought became "I don't bite the hook anymore; I'm not a stupid fish!"

[AE: *Terry London shows in these transcripts how REBT can be nicely used with a 10-year-old boy. He quickly gains rapport with the boy; discovers the "rough spot" that bothers him (kids making fun of him); gets his agreement to shrink it down; shows him "the way we think is the way we feel"; shows him how to change his feelings by using "cool thoughts" in the form of rational coping statements; illustrates how if he stops biting the hook that other kids put out for him, he will stop reinforcing their teasing; gets the boy to use a tape recorder to practice thinking aloud his cool thoughts; and role-plays the bully while the client practices his relaxing exercises and cool thoughts while reacting to the bully.*

All told, Terry London uses a variety of REBT methods and adapts them to a 10-year-old boy without really teaching him how to do active disputing, as would be appropriate to use with an older child. Showing the client how to use cool thoughts or rational coping statements works really well.]

A 15-Year-Old Girl With Anger and Low Frustration Tolerance

Therapist: Marie Joyce, Ph.D.

This case is with "Cara," a 15-year-old girl who was referred by her teacher because of adjustment difficulties that were interfering with her life in a number of ways. Intense conflict was being experienced with her mother at home and poor concentration was disrupting her schoolwork. Preceding the interview described below was a brief introductory session exploring the nature and seriousness of the problems and explaining the kind of therapy being offered. Cara was introduced to the advantage of reflecting on her thoughts and beliefs and of rating associated feelings.

The aim in this session was to assess Cara's emotions and beliefs and to begin disputation to help her to calm herself down. Problem-solving about the practical problems could come later.

ETHICAL ISSUE

Psychologists who are teachers and supervisors of trainee psychologists and professional colleagues have a long tradition of using case material to enhance their activities. This has traditionally occurred in classroom teaching, in individual and group supervision, in professional workshops, and in written works such as books. In utilizing case material for purposes of teaching and learning, ethical issues arise, including protection of the confidentiality of the person involved. In recent decades much more emphasis has been placed on psychologists obtaining informed consent of clients, although practitioner/educators draw constantly on clinical experience to illustrate points of teaching, particularly in subjects such as clinical assessment and interventions. A chapter such as the present one involves more than a brief mention of an individual, as it includes a full interview with the young person. The case reported here is one I recorded more than ten years ago. It was recorded on audio cassette with permission, for teaching and learning purposes, and identifying data was removed. The identity of the client is now lost over time so the interview material has been utilized in this book on the basis of earlier consent as no current follow up has been possible.

(Assessing the A 's, or Adversities)

THERAPIST: Tell me about you and your mother this week.

CLIENT: I normally help babysitting and I help around the house and everything. But this weekend . . . I wanted to do something. I didn't want to sit at home for the whole weekend. And then she started on . . . I think she was in a bad mood to start with and so she just put up all these things and we ended up in a big argument and I thought, "Oh, keep calm and not go off my head, because then I'm not going to get anywhere."

T: Yes.

C: What she's saying . . . it's true to some point but it's not true that I don't do anything. I do do things around the house. I'm not "just lazy" as she's saying.

(Assessing the C's, or Consequences)

T: Right. Cara, what was the feeling that you had, the strongest feeling? Was it a feeling of anger when she was not letting you go out and then criticizing you, or was it a feeling of upset and anxiety? What was the main feeling?

C: I was angry but I was upset as well because it wasn't fair—because I was doing things . . . I was helping around the house. If she was having a hard day or something because my little brother was sick, why take it out on me? And say "No, you can't go out" . . . because she was having some sort of hassles.

T: So you were thinking to yourself that it really wasn't fair the way she was treating you, and you were feeling quite upset about that.

C: Yes.

T: How upset were you feeling? In terms of 0 to 10? You know . . . the Feeling Thermometer we spoke about last time!

C: About 7 or 8.

T: About 7 or 8. So you were pretty upset that she was treating you so unfairly.

C: Yes.

T: Mmm. And did it last very long?

C: Well, we had an argument for about an hour in the morning, and I just ended up going shopping. I thought, "I'm just going . . . I'm not going to bother trying to finish it." And then I saw her later on in the afternoon. Then she started up again. And umm . . . like when I went shopping and I was doing other things, I didn't really think about it, but then when I got back home, and when she was complaining and everything, I could see it was going to start all over again. Then it got to a point where I was really getting mad and really upset, 'cause all I wanted was to go out for a few hours for the night. And then it just got time for me to leave and I just thought, "I'm going to go."

T: And you went?

C: And I went. Yes . . . But the thing is whenever I go out, because I always end up going out when she says "No, I don't really want you to. I don't want you to go out." 'Cause any time I go out I get the same thing all over again. So I always feel like I've hassled all my way to get to go out, and then by the time I go out I just feel totally drained of everything. I think "Is it all worth it for just going out for, say, three hours?" I feel a little bit . . . I don't know . . . I don't feel guilty . . . I just . . . I really . . . I just feel like maybe I shouldn't. Maybe I should just stay home. It's not worth it. But then that all passes over. I get all confused.

T: I think you get confused because you have a lot of feelings.

C: Mmmm.

(Seeking to prioritize the C's)

T: We often feel confused when we have many different feelings at once. Out of all those feelings, which would be the worst problem for you? Is it the anger or the upset or the guilt or . . . ?

C: I think it's the upset because it's . . . 'cause I don't think I'm being unreasonable. I mean I don't ask to stay out till all hours of the morning and I don't ask to go out that often . . . I mean . . . but maybe two or three times a month I'll ask to go out at night, 'cause usually during the day it's no problem.

(Assessing the B's, or Beliefs)

T: Okay. So here's "reasonable you" asking your Mum for a reasonable amount of outings.

C: Mmmm.

T: And you put in a reasonable amount of study, and you put in a reasonable amount of helping in the house. And here's Mum being unreasonable with you!

C: (laughs) Yes!

T: Right? And she shouldn't be unreasonable with you!

C: Mmm.

T: She should be fair!

C: Mmm.

(Disputing)

T: Is that true?

C: . . . Idealistic!

T: Idealistic. Yes. So when I reflect back to you how you are thinking, you are starting to see already that it's a bit of idealistic thinking. Okay. So you are already beginning to dispute in your own mind whether that's really true.

C: Yes.

T: What you are saying to yourself—that she should be fair? She always—totally and all the time—100 percent—should be fair. (Pause) Why is that not true?

C: (pause) Because she's not perfect.

(Bringing in some humor)

T: Because she's not perfect! (Laughter) Because she isn't perfect. But shouldn't she be perfect?

C: (pause) . . . When I want to go out, she should be! (Laughs)

T: Yes. When you want to go out she should be. So when you want something you should get it! . . . . If it's fair and reasonable and . . .

C: Whatever! (laughs)

T: Okay. Now is that really the way life is?

C: No.

T: No. It's not. But a lot of the time we tell ourselves such things and we believe things should be perfect or that we should get treated fairly when we want to be treated fairly. So what we are doing is changing our wants and wishes and preferences into demands. Is that right?

C: Yes.

T: Instead of just thinking, "Well I really wish she'd be fair and I really want her to treat me fairly and reasonably and sensibly," we say, "She should treat me fairly! She mustn't treat me like this!"

C: Mmm.

(Therapist wants to assess anger further)

T: Can you see that absolute MUST coming in?

C: Yes.

T: Now what happens when we think that absolute *must*—that she must treat me fairly, she must treat me reasonably and . . .

C: We get disappointed 'cause it doesn't happen.

T: We get disappointed 'cause it doesn't happen, but what else do we get? We get more than disappointed. We get . . . ?

(No response from C.)

What's the feeling you have when she says, "You don't even help around the house!"

C: Angry.

T: Angry. Right. You get angry. If we're feeling angry at someone it's because we're making a demand, an unreasonable, irrational demand of them that they be different from what they are, that is, imperfect human beings.

C: Yes.

T: But if we're just wishing that they were reasonable human beings at a time when they're not being, if we wish and prefer it, then we are going to be just disappointed and frustrated. Is that right? But can we be disappointed and frustrated without being too upset?

C: *(uncertainly)* Yeah, I guess so.

T: Is that true or not? You think about that for a minute. Have you sometimes experienced being disappointed and frustrated about something but not been too upset?

C: (indecipherable)

T: Not too sure about that? Okay. Well let's go back to the angry feelings. Do you want to feel less angry? Does your anger help you or hurt you?

C: It hurts.

T: It hurts you. How does it hurt you?

C: It makes it worse. It makes it worse.

T: Yes. How does it make it worse?

C: Interferes with rational thought, I guess.

T: Yes, and what tends to happen? What happened for an hour on Saturday?

C: Arguments.

(Disputation using the negative consequences of the angry emotion)

T: Arguments, plus! So that when people are angry they tend to fight and attack each other and blame each other . . . You know, our behavior gets worse, doesn't it, when we are angry? We can feel churned up and tight and our blood starts to really "boil." Is that doing us much good?

C: No.

T: It doesn't help us and it hurts us to get very, very angry a lot. It doesn't help the situation and it doesn't help us getting along with people. So there are two good reasons for giving up some of our anger . . . Is that right?

C: Yes.

T: Yes. How angry would you say you were getting on Saturday?

C: Really, really angry.

T: Were you? So it was even higher than the 7 or 8 upset? Whereabouts was it on the scale of 0 to 10?

C: Up to 9.

T: So the anger might be more of a problem than the upset, 'cause it's stronger isn't it, or a bit stronger?

C: Yes.

(Employing Rational Emotive Imagery to dispute irrational beliefs underlying anger)

T: Okay. (pause) Now, let's try using some imagery to help you change how you feel about something obnoxious happening, 'cause no-one's going to say that putting up with that is a "bed of roses." Okay? It's unpleasant, it's not what you want. It's unreasonable at times, it's Mum in a bad mood, or got something up her nose, or someone else . . . you know, and you're copping it. That's not pleasant! No one's saying "Oh that's lovely for you! That's great, Cara! Why don't you enjoy it?" No. it's a pain! . . . Okay . . . So let's use imaginary pictures . . . What I want you to do is just shut your eyes for a few minutes and picture yourself in detail back at Saturday again: Here's Mum, and you've just said "Mum, I've been thinking about tonight and, um, I'm planning to go out for a few hours," and Mum starts! "You never help around the house! I never get any help from you at all. What sort of daughter are you?" and on she goes . . . Just keep your eyes closed and just get yourself feeling that feeling of anger all over again. I want you to really feel that anger. Okay, just nod your head when you can feel that anger again. Take your time. I want you to really be able to feel it . . . Just really angry with her for how she was treating you unfairly . . . feel that anger.

C: Mmm.

T: Now I want you to take your time but to change that feeling of strong, really strong anger to just frustration and disappointment. Instead of being really, really angry at her, you're sorry she's treating you like this. You're disappointed. You're frustrated. Can you feel that now?

C: Yes.

T: Okay. Now, when you are ready, open your eyes and tell me, how did you change those feelings?

C: I told myself to keep calm. (pause) And that she is just in a bad mood.

T: So . . . she's just in a bad mood—there's a reason, a good reason why she's behaving the way she is. Yes. Anything else?

C: There's no point in getting angry over this 'cause it's not going to make it any better.

T: Yes. There's no point in the anger. It's not going to make it any better. (pause) That's about it? Did you think any other thoughts? That's good, very good because that really worked to get you to change that anger into disappointment and frustration, which are healthy negative emotions for what's happening, aren't they? They are not the exaggerated, unhealthy anger. Perhaps you could also think about your 'must'—changing your 'must' into a wish or a preference, instead of thinking "She mustn't treat me so unfairly," you could think "I wish she wasn't treating me like this."

C: Yes.

(Getting to the beliefs underlying her Low Frustration Tolerance)

T: "Even though it's not fair and I don't like it, I can stand it!"

C: (laughs) Right!

T: Is that right? Is that a good one?

C: Yes.

T: Yes, because what do we generally think when people are treating us unfairly? "They shouldn't treat me unfairly, but when they do it's awful and I can't stand it." Is that sometimes what you think?

C: Yes.

(Disputing the Low Frustration Tolerance irrational beliefs)

T: Is that really true?

C: No.

T: How do you know?

C: I'm still here!

T: 'Cause you're still here!

C: I'm still standing it!

T: You're still standing it and you've probably been standing it for a long time.

C: Mmm.

T: But if we put up with things and we stand them for a long time, unpleasant though they be, but at the same time we're telling ourselves, "I can't stand this!" how are we going to be feeling?

C: Tense and uptight.

T: Yes. Really tense and uptight and much more upset.

C: Mmm.

(Disputing and working to strengthen rational beliefs)

T: Because if we are being asked to stand something that's unbearable—that's pretty upsetting, isn't it? That's pretty bad? Yeah. Whereas if we look at it realistically that even though it's a pain in the bum we can stand it—we're going to feel calmer about it—and frustrated, but deal with it . . . as something obnoxious but tolerable. Okay. So just go over that now because there's a lot there that's really important. These are the thoughts that are going to help you not just believe it lightly, which you do at the moment, but get you to believe it really strongly—that you can stand it.

C: It's just that when you are really . . . in the middle of a fight, you don't think "I can stand this!"

T: At the moment you don't! But with practice you can get into the habit of doing that and not getting into as many fights. The imagery exercise is something that

I want you to do, not just now but every day. To spend a few minutes every day practicing this. It's a mental rehearsal, a technique that we call rational-emotive imagery because you are using your thoughts to control your emotions and feelings and you are using images, pictures of what's happening. So if you use this imagery method, you can learn to be more in charge of your own feelings, more emotionally responsible. Then when something happens, you've got a repertoire of different ways you can feel and you can have ready a calmer, more sensible way of thinking about what's happened, instead of the automatic knee-jerk anger and "she mustn't treat me like this," "I can't stand it," "It's not fair" . . . that you've already got in your repertoire and you've practiced and rehearsed. Thinking "Ah well, there she goes again. Don't like this. Never going to like this but I know I can stand it." Okay? Now it doesn't happen with just one or two practices, because . . . why doesn't it happen like that?

C: Do you think—because you're not used to responding in that way?

T: That's right. You've got very strong habits the other way.

C: Yes.

T: It takes quite a bit of work to overcome it. In fact, some people would go so far as to say we have a biological tendency to actually think crookedly!

C: Oh.

(Introducing homework)

T: And it does certainly seem to come more easily to us. If you look around at people in your family, and friends you know, and yourself at times, it seems as though it's much easier for us to think in a stupid, irrational way than it is to think sensibly and calmly. So it takes even more effort. So you can practice the imagery each day and next time we can review both your feelings and how you are managing the different situations at home

C: Okay.

[AE: *This is an excellent second session with a 15-year-old girl who is angry at her mother's "unfair" criticism. Marie Joyce, as is usual in REBT,* assumes *that the girl is* right *about describing her mother's unfairness and does not question her description. REBT holds that even if her mother was unfair, Cara would not have to choose to be very angry at her, but instead could merely make herself feel quite frustrated and disappointed, which are* healthy *negative feelings when something "unfairly" goes wrong in her life. So the therapist helps Cara see that she largely made herself angry at her mother and that she can also make herself disappointed at her mother's behavior but not incensed at* her, *the whole behaving* person.

I would object slightly to the therapist, in using rational-emotive imagery, instructing Cara to "Get that feeling of anger all over again." I would paint the grim picture she paints for Cara and then ask, "How do you now feel?" Cara might respond that she feels very angry; but she might instead say she now feels guilty or self-blaming. So in REBT, the therapist, using rational-emotive imagery, paints a grim picture but does not *prescribe an unhealthy negative feeling. Rather she does prescribe a healthy negative feeling to replace the unhealthy one that the client comes up with.*

Marie Joyce otherwise does fine REBT with Cara, and apparently helps her considerably to see how she can choose *her feelings when her mother—or anyone else—threats her unfairly.*]

CASE

4

A 10-Year-Old Boy Whining About Dogs in His Home

Therapist: Albert Ellis, Ph.D.

"Joey," a 10-year-old boy, was brought to see me because he kept whining about animals in his home and because his parents "couldn't stand" his whining. He had seen me three times before because, although bright and capable, he was not doing his schoolwork; that had greatly improved but now he had a new problem.

CLIENT: We've got two dogs, a cat, and they constantly fight and I constantly break it up and I constantly get mad.

THERAPIST: Yeah. Well, what good is it doing you to get mad?

C: No good. It just relieves the tension.

T: Does it?

C: Yes.

T: When I saw you last time you weren't doing work in school, right?

C: School is perfectly all right. I've been doing okay in school.

T: So that's no problem anymore. You're doing your work in school and getting along all right and you're just whining about only the animals. Is that the only thing?

C: There's really nothing else.

T: Yeah. Well, if you are right and it does relieve the tension, why don't you whine to yourself?

C: Because it doesn't relieve the tension as much.

T: Well, I think you're probably wrong about that, because if you whine to your mother then she's going to get after you, and then there's going to be more tension. Isn't that right?

C: True.

T: Well, if you went out and whined to yourself, or for that matter to your friends, assuming that your friends would take it, then it would be okay with your mother and then presumably you'd be better off. Though, if your mother could take it, as I suppose she could, then it wouldn't be the worst thing in the world to whine at her. Who's around when you do it? Just your mother? Or who else?

C: My mother. That's really it.

T: Where's your father when this is going on?

C: Usually at work.

T: So he doesn't hear much of it.

C: He hears a lot even though . . .

T: He what?

C: He hears a lot even though he's at work.

T: Oh, I see. And how does he feel about it?

C: I really don't know.

T: He doesn't say anything?

C: He doesn't say anything to me.

T: So, he probably gets after your mother to get after you.

C: I wouldn't know.

T: That's what usually happens. Fathers frequently don't do anything directly with the children but they do say to the mother, "Why don't you stop that brat from whining?" So I suspect that is what's happening. What does your mother normally do when you whine too much?

C: Yell.

T: And then what do you do?

C: Then I walk away.

T: But how do you feel when you walk away after she yells.

C: Not good.

T: You see, that's what I said. It doesn't cause any great feelings all around. You could say to yourself, "There goes my crazy mother whining back at me." Say that and that would reduce your whining a little or somewhat. But generally speaking, your whining is not going to make a good situation, and she's probably going to do you in if you keep this up. Isn't she?

C: Yeah.

T: Yeah, that's a problem. So you're really not gaining. Why does she have so many animals?

C: Well, we had a dog, a cat, you know, who were quiet all the time and then you know our house got burgularized . . . bur-gu-lar. . . . You know what I mean.

T: Burglarized.

C: Right. Something like that.

T: That's a lousy word.

C: Three times. And the dog slept through it. So, we wanted to get a real good watchdog and this watchdog is not a watchdog. She barks at everything and constantly. . . . She's not housebroken, she's a puppy. The dogs don't get along, they fight, the cat scratches the dogs.

T: How many dogs are there?

C: Two.

T: The watchdog and the other one.

C: Right.

T: And those two don't get along.

C: No, they hate each other.

T: And how many cats?

C: Four.

T: And are they all in the same. . . . Is it a house that you live in?

C: Yeah.

T: How big is the house?

C: Three floors.

T: Three floors. Who takes care of the animals?

C: Everyone. We have to walk them like once every hour for 15 minutes.

T: And you don't enjoy that?

C: No, no one does.

T: Well . . . wait a minute . . . just let me get this straight. The only ones that get walked are the dogs?

C: Right.

T: You don't walk the cats?

C: Well, the cats make on the floor, to make up for everything, so . . .

T: You eliminated talking about them?

C: No. See, they make on the floor . . .

T: So, who has to clean it up?

C: My mother, because she sees it and I don't even know what it looks like. Because the only way she can tell is when the cats wet the rug.

T: I see. So that's not your problem, the cat. Your problem is with the dog?

C: No, but the cat makes my mother, you know . . . get mad and then the dogs fight, which makes my mother get madder. So after a while she gets on me.

T: Yeah, I see. Well, a better solution for the whole thing probably would be get rid of the dogs and get one good dog.

C: Yeah, that would be a quite good situation.

T: Well, why doesn't your mother do that?

C: There's no way we can get rid of the dogs.

T: What do you mean . . . you can give 'em away. You can get rid of dogs.

C: No. We happen to be a very humane family. We don't give away dogs.

T: Well, what's so humane about giving yourself a pain in the ass? I'm not clear about that.

C: There isn't, but we just don't get rid of any. My mother picks up dogs that are lying down in the street, because you know. . . . We had this dog a couple of weeks ago that we found, it was ill, you know. We had to bring it to the vet.

T: Yeah?

C: But later we found its owner so we gave it back.

T: But had you not found the owner you would have kept the dog?

C: No.

T: Well, what would you have done with it?

C: We have no idea, but we couldn't keep three dogs.

T: That's the point. I don't think it's wise to keep two.

C: It isn't.

T: Even if you got rid of the old dog and kept the new watchdog.

C: No. No. No. No, we definitely should get rid of the watchdog and keep the old dog.

T: Then the robberies would start again.

C: Well, it's better to lose a little money then lose the whole family's sanity.

T: Well, you would insist on losing your sanity if you got rid of the old dog? You would *make yourself* lose your sanity by telling yourself you were *no good* for getting rid of it.

C: No, but that means we'd have the little dog, the puppy, which is not a puppy. She's a great big German Shepherd. We'd still lose our sanity because she barks at everything, she runs around, she eats everything, she bothers the cat, the cat scratches her.

T: Wait. That's the new dog?

C: Right.

T: How long have you had her? *Her* is right?

C: Yeah.

T: How long have you had her?

C: I'd say around three months.

T: And it doesn't look like she's going to get any better?

C: No wait. Three months. Six months.

T: It doesn't look like she's going to get any better, does it?

C: Well, she's only a puppy right now. She's only eight months old. We got her when she was two months.

T: I know. But does that kind of dog get better?

C: I really can't tell you that. I have never had one.

T: Well, can't you find out from the vet or something?

C: Well, the reason she's biting is because, you know . . . She likes for me to get her a rawhide, but you know she chews through that in less than a day.

T: There must be better dogs.

C: Not at all.

T: And you're saying that even if somebody gave you one, you wouldn't get rid of the pain-in-the-ass dog. Is that right?

C: Yes, sir. Is my mother coming up here? (Joey's mother was waiting for him downstairs in our reception area.)

T: I don't know. Is she supposed to?

C: I really couldn't say. I don't really want her to.

T: You don't want her to?

C: No.

T: Because I'll get her to come upstairs if you want. I'll tell her, too, the same thing I'm telling you.

C: No, really, I don't want her here at all.

T: Okay. You don't want me to bring her upstairs. But that would be the best solution that I can think of. It would first be to change both dogs.

C: Yeah well . . . I don't know.

T: And that's what I would recommend. But if you are not going to do that, let's suppose you're going to keep this nutty situation going. Then the second best solution would be to go whine as much as you want in the bathroom or in the cellar or somewhere, but not to your mother because it's just not going to pay off. Your mother's enough of a pain in the ass, isn't she?

C: Yeah.

T: And she's going to be worse if you whine. So, you can (a) whine silently to yourself and say "F—— it! f—— it! f—— it!" or whatever you want to say. Or (b) even if you whine loudly, you could do it in the cellar or someplace else. Do you have a cellar?

C: Yeah.

T: So why don't you go down in the cellar and whine?

C: Because I never thought of it.

T: You see, because this way you're going to make things worse. You're really trying to bother your mother. Maybe you're trying to give her a pain in the ass.

C: No.

T: Are you sure about that?

C: I'm positive about it.

T: All right then. As I said, with your nutty mother, you'd be wiser if you continued doing what you're doing but not aloud. Because now you've got the dogs and the cats and your mother after you. See, the other way, without your whining, you'd only have the dogs and the cats, which are bad enough; and maybe it will get better. Maybe. But I don't know about that dog. I'm skeptical. I think you just got the wrong dog. I don't even think that it's probably the species of dog, I think it's that particular dog. The species is probably all right. German Shepherds are usually okay. But this one sounds like a wild pain in the ass and I doubt if it's ever going to work out. If you were really wise, you would just get rid of the damn dog and get another one. In fact, get rid of both dogs and get another one. But if you don't want to do that, and you're entitled to do whatever you want, then you better live with them. Let's see what whining generally is. Do you realize what you are telling yourself when you whine?

C: No.

T: Well, any time a human being gets disturbed about anything in the universe, whatever the hell it is, and we're not talking about being annoyed or irritated or sad or regretful. You see, when something goes wrong in the universe—somebody gives you a pain in the ass, a friend, a teacher, your mother, your father, the dogs—normally you would tell yourself, "That's a pain in the ass. I don't like it. I wish it weren't so. What a nuisance!" Right? That's what you'd say to yourself, whether you said it to other people or not. Isn't that right? Now if you stuck with those statements, how would you feel? "That's a pain in the ass! I don't like it. What a nuisance. But that's the way it is." How would you feel?

C: I really don't know.

T: You'd feel sorry and regretful and annoyed and irritated. And those would be healthy negative feelings, because they would help you to try to get rid of the pain in the ass. I guarantee that if I were in your place right now I'd be saying, "S——. This is a crummy situation. Let's see what I can do about it." And I would try to change the dogs. Because you see, if something went wrong in the universe and you said to yourself, "I like it," that's nutty, isn't it? Or, if you said to yourself, "Well. Who gives a god——. I'm indifferent to it." That's nutty, isn't it? So the healthy statement, when something is painful, is to say to yourself, "What a pain in the a——! How obnoxious! I don't like it! What can I do to remove this?" If a thorn were in your foot and you were indifferent to it, it wouldn't do you much good, would it?

C: No.

T: You see. So, "I don't like it," is a healthy negative thing to say to yourself. When we say that to ourselves, we feel sorry and regretful and annoyed. Now if the thing is very, very bad, if your closest friend dies, then you say, "That's really most unfortunate," and you even feel sorrier. You feel the *n*th degree of sadness or irritation if a big thing goes wrong. Well, if the dogs, for example, are only mean once in awhile. . . .

C: They aren't once in awhile.

T: Well, but if they were, you'd feel mildly sad. Sorrow and regret range from 0 to 100. And in your case it sounds like an 80 or 90 percent. So if you would healthfully think, "Damn it, I don't like this at all!" You would feel about 80 or 90 percent sorry. Very sorry. But you also feel angry. Whining is really anger. You feel upset and you may even feel depressed. Now, anger is more than annoyance. It's quite different. It means, in addition to "I don't like this. What a pain in the ass! I wish it weren't so. Let's see what we can do about it," you're saying, "It's awful! I can't stand it! It shouldn't be that way!" Do you see the difference? All disturbance includes a "should" or a "must," such as, "Because it's so bad, the damn dogs, it shouldn't be that way." That's whining. Now do you see why that's nutty? Why?

C: Just that it's quite stupid to complain. Well, seeing what you just told me right now—that if I complain to my mother—she gets even madder and then she gets on your nerves even more.

T: Right. And also suppose you didn't even have a mother. Suppose you just lived in the house alone with the dog. Let's just suppose it to make it simple. If you are saying, "Damn it, this is the worst situation I ever saw," that might be correct. But as soon as you say, "Therefore it shouldn't be that way," you become Godlike. You say, "Because I don't like it, it shouldn't exist." Now that's horses——, because no matter how much you don't like a thing, there is no reason it *shouldn't* exist. It does exist, you see. Every time a person says, "It must not exist!" or "It should not exist!" he's really crazy because he's saying that the way the universe is, shouldn't be! "I run the universe and it shouldn't be the way it is!" Or "There is a law of the universe that says it shouldn't exist that way for me." Well, that's nonsense. Whatever exists, exists. Suppose somebody were torturing you to death, let's just suppose that, and you were whining about it. Then you'd be saying to yourself "They *shouldn't* be torturing me!" Well, why shouldn't they be torturing you? It's most, most unfortunate that the worse thing is happening to you—torture to death. It would be hard to think of anything worse. But it's still silly to say, "Because it's the worse thing that can happen to me and because it's unfair, it shouldn't be!" Because *it is*. Humans beings are crazy for whining because they're always demanding, not wishing or wanting good situations to exist, which is okay. You don't *want* those dogs to be that way.

C: No.

T: If you could really wave a magic wand and get rid of the watchdog, you'd get rid of her. But you are saying, "Because I don't want her to act like that, she *must not* act that way!" Well, there's nothing that *must not* be. No matter how bad it is. If you are dying of cancer, you are dying of cancer. That's tough s———. That's the way it is. There's no use whining about it. You might not be happy about it. That would be nutty. Or being indifferent is crazy. But whining is a demand. It's not a desire. Desires are fine. You could desire, for example, to have a million dollars. But if you don't have it, it's crazy to say, "I should have a million dollars because I desire it." Isn't it?

C: Yeah. It is crazy.

T: Yeah. So every time human beings whine, they're demanding, they're not wanting. A whine is a silly demand, an expectation of the universe. "It must be the way I want it!" And even if nobody heard you whining, you would still be crazy. If the Martians ever come down here, they'll think we're all nuts. Because human beings are born whiners. They don't just feel sorrow, feel regretful and annoyed when things are lousy, which is a good thing because then they can work to change them. But when they can't change them, then they whine about it. Right now you don't think you can change the situation. I think you probably could. Because the other reason why whining is no good is because it doesn't have action. The more you whine, the less you really do anything about it. If I were living in your condition, I wouldn't be whining at all but I'd be determined to get rid of those dogs to change the situation. Come hell or high water. Because who needs this? It's a pain in the a———. Now, you could say it's cruel to the dogs to get rid of them. But I think it's probably better to be somewhat unkind to dogs than to be cruel to humans. You've got a choice. Suppose the dogs were really biting you all the time. What would you do?

C: Well. They don't bite at all, but I'd give 'em a shot, you know, right in the mouth.

T: That's right or finally you'd get rid of them. Suppose they kept biting. Every time they recovered from your shot in the mouth they kept biting. You'd get rid of them. Well, I don't think they're biting, but they are certainly annoying. They sound very annoying. I think you and your mother and father are self-defeating for keeping them. Because it's true you're being kind to the dogs but you're also being unkind to you. Humans better be a little bit more kind to themselves than to animals, plants, and trees. . . . Because by taking kindness to extremes, you can say, "Well, we must not even kill cattle," but the reason we kill cattle is because we eat. It's too damn bad that we kill cattle but it's better that we can choose to kill cattle and stay alive by eating them. So if you're wise you may say, "That's the way the world is. It's either the cattle or me, so I prefer to kill the cattle. It's not the greatest thing in the world, and it's a tough decision to make. That's the way the universe is. Just like the lion kills the hare. The lion isn't cruel for killing the hare. The world is so arranged that unless the lion kills the hare, the lion doesn't eat. It's foolish to say the lion is cruel. Many animals kill some other animal. It's not the greatest way in the world, you know, but that's what you'd better do, if you are a lion. Even little animals eat ants and other animals. It's not cruel because unfortunately the universe is arranged that way. Someday we'll invent a better universe where nothing gets killed, but we haven't managed to do that yet, and who the hell knows if we ever will. In the meantime, we eat chicken, we eat cattle, etc. And if dogs are too much of a pain in the ass, we get rid of them. And I would advise you and your family to get rid of those dogs. Give them away. Go get another dog. But if you're not going to do that, then it's silly to be whining, because whining really says, "Because I don't like it, it should not exist. I should run the f—— universe." That's what a whine really says and, "It's *awful* that things are not the way I want them to be!" Awful means it's badder than it must be! "I can't stand it!" Well, that's nonsense. You do stand it. See, no matter how bad a thing is, you're obviously standing it. If you drop dead, you won't stand it but as long as you're alive, you do. So, anytime a person upsets herself, and you can watch it with your mother, for example—she gets upset a lot, right?—if you watch what's going on, you'll see she's saying things to herself: (1) "Something stinks," and (2) "It shouldn't!" You don't get upset without that nutty "shouldn't." The first statement, "Something stinks" may be right. She says, "My son is whining and that stinks." Well, from her point of view, that's correct. But then, "He *shouldn't* be whining!" Well, that's crazy. Why *shouldn't* you be? It would be *nice* if you weren't, but you are. She's not accepting reality. Every time we get upset we say reality *shouldn't* be the way it is. We refuse to accept it. So if you were wise, you'd look at your own whining, even if it wasn't loud and nobody heard it.

I am very direct, forceful, and sometimes even a little dogmatic in this part of the session with Joey—more than I would be with many 10-year-old children—for several reasons:

1. I saw him for a few previous sessions about his not doing his school work, and found that he was amenable to forceful REBT. In fact, when I at first was relatively gentle with him, we got nowhere. He still kept rebelling against his teachers and parents. I only helped him change his self-defeating behavior by very firmly showing him how he was foolishly sabotaging *himself* with his kind of short-range rebellion, and that he would almost certainly continue to get poor results if he kept it up. I hard-headedly demonstrated that even if his parents and teachers were wrong and unfair, his manner of defying them was foolishly interfering with his *own* goals and desires. My firm use of REBT with Joey finally worked, and he improved remarkably in his homework.

2. Even in our original sessions, and also in this new session, I sized up Joey as a "tough" and relatively invulnerable kid who could take my firmness and my

rough language, respect it, and probably benefit from it. With many children who are vulnerable and conventional, I would have put my REBT teachings into milder, more tactful language.

3. I often am very direct and "rough" with children right from the start of therapy, to see how they react to my down-to-earth disputing of their Irrational Beliefs and my urging them to construct more Rational Beliefs and behaviors. If they take well to my directness and language, fine. If at first it appears to be too much for them, I quickly tone it down and use a quieter form of REBT. Each client reacts differently, and I diagnose how well or how poorly clients react by experimenting with "rougher" and "gentler" language to see which works best for each one.

C: Another reason I came here is, one day she found a couple of notes that, you know, I was only kidding around, the kids and I, you know, class were only kidding around and they were really perverted notes.

T: Saying what? What did one of them say?

C: I don't even remember.

T: Did you write in the notes that you wanted to do some so-called perverted kind of sex?

C: Nah. It was really, really stupid but my mother really got upset.

T: But what does she think it means? That you're going to *do* something?

C: No. She knows that, you know. But she immediately went to the person that I wrote it to.

T: Another fellow, or what?

C: No. It was with a girl.

T: How old is the girl?

C: My age.

T: Yeah.

C: And, you know, she started talking to her mother. The girl's mother got upset at her and, you know, it just caused a great, you know. . . .

T: Well, they're acting pretty nuttily. They don't understand it. Whatever you wrote along those lines, in all probability, is very normal as long as they're only notes. As long you just imagine it and think about it. As long as you're not going to rape the girl . . .

C: I don't even think about it.

T: . . . or do anything else. So, they're just making a big case out of it. They're being nutty. People are. They're very crazy about sex; and, again, your mother is telling herself the same two things: (1) "You did the wrong thing." Which is a little correct, because in our stupid society, you don't write those kind of notes.

You write them to yourself but you don't . . . You actually gave it to the girl, didn't you?

C: Yeah, but it was just fun; and, you know, she wrote back and, you know, the whole class was doing it.

T: How did your mother find it?

C: It was in my desk.

T: Well, you see, that was a mistake. So (1) your mother is saying: "Joey did the wrong thing." For by her standards, it was wrong. And (2) she's telling herself, "How *awful*! He *shouldn't* have done that. There's something very rotten about it and about him for doing it." So, she's making herself upset. But even if she was right, which she doesn't have to be in this case, that you did the wrong thing—so screw it, so you did the wrong thing—she's making herself upset, she's damning you, she's saying it's horrible, when it isn't. It's a wrong thing to do at worst. But if you watch that you'll see that every time your mother, or your father, or your friends make themselves upset, they're always saying nutty things. They're telling themselves some crazy "shouldn't." Either that they *shouldn't* do something, in which case they feel depressed and anxious, or that somebody else shouldn't do it, in which case they feel angry, whiny. Or, that the world *shouldn't* be that way, the way it is, in which case again, they whine about the universe. If human beings were wise, they'd stop their absolutistic "shouldn'ts," and still they wouldn't like what goes on in the world because it often stinks. But that's the way it is. Tough. And the less you whine, the more you can do. Whining takes time and energy, usually leads to other people—like your mother—getting upset, and it doesn't get you what you really want. What a waste of time! If, instead of whining, you spent more time and energy plotting and scheming how to change the dog situation, that would be much better. Even, for example, you do have a cellar in your home?

C: Yeah.

T: Why shouldn't the dogs practically always stay in the cellar?

C: One of the dogs we lock up a little, you know . . . Lots of the time she gets mad. We have to take her out sometimes.

T: What about the other dog?

C: The other dog roams free.

T: What?

C: The other dog roams free. Can go wherever she wants.

T: The big one?

C: The puppy stays in the little, you know, the little corner.

T: But there are other systems, you know. You do have land around your home, or what?

C: No.

T: Is there land there?

C: Yeah. We have a backyard but we don't have it fenced in.

T: Why don't you fence it in?

C: I have no idea.

T: See, that's another solution.

C: It's not my money to spend.

T: But that would save you so much time and energy. It really would. You could get wire and put it up yourself. You see. That's what I said. If you stop whining, you figure out solutions. Probably all you have to do is fence in your backyard, and you have a yard. Fences have special exits and entrances for dogs. . . . You know what they are?

C: Yeah. You put one of those things on the door that you push in and out.

T: And you can fix up one of those so the dog can get out, at times, but not in. You see. So when you're not home the dog can get out but sometimes it can't get back in or sometimes it can. If you fix it up in a certain way so that the dog will be very little trouble, the dog wouldn't bother you at all. And it seems to be much cheaper to fence your yard in. Is it a big yard?

C: Well, I would say 15 by 20.

T: That isn't very large. You could fence that in. And it doesn't have to be a high fence, so that people couldn't get in. That isn't the problem. It's just a fence big enough to stop the dog.

C: The dog can jump quite high.

T: Well, all right, but you could put wire up. Well, the dog can't jump too high.

C: Well, actually he can jump six foot. He can jump past my head.

T: So you put up an eight-foot fence. Or, you put a wire over the top of the fence. You could fix it so the dog won't jump it. So, something like that. Once you stop the whining you figure out ways to do things, while the whining really interrupts your thinking process. You say to yourself, "Oh this is terrible, this is awful, isn't it horrible." Then you don't accept it and work to change it.

C: Okay. Would you like to speak with my mother though?

T: Well, we are only going to have a couple of minutes . . .

C: I don't care if you speak with her or not.

T: Yeah. Well, there probably isn't going to be enough time. But you tell her that if she is upset and she wants to come in and talk to me about the problem, I'll be glad to give her her own session. Because it's going to take 20 minutes, at least, for me to go over things with her, and I'll tell her some of the things I told you that would better change the situation.

C: Okay.

T: Okay. You go think about it.

I thought that I would have to see Joey several times before I would be able to convince him to reduce his whining and that I probably would have to see his mother as well. To my surprise, however, his mother came to see me a month later and said, "I don't know what you did with Joey, but it's almost a miracle. He still hates the dogs but he's been whining very little about them. I would say that he's putting up with them beautifully."

I told her what I told Joey, and she understood it and was glad that it was working. I spoke with her about possible changing the dog situation, but I saw that Joey was right. She wouldn't in the least consider changing things. I had much more difficulty with her than I had with her son. In spite of her kindness to and tolerance with animals, she was often very angry with Joey, with her husband, and several other members of her husband's family, about how absolutely wrong they were about politics, religion, and practically everything they did. I tried to rationally convince her that, yes, they all might be wrong but, if so, they *should* and *must*—at least at the moment—be wrong. No luck. She rigidly stuck to her "righteous" anger and kept uselessly fighting with them.

My conclusion? Joey was probably what I call a "nice neurotic" and was rebellious about the family's dogs. His mother, alas, suffered from a severe personality disorder and resisted all my and other people's efforts to help her change. After all, right is right! I succeeded with Joey in a few sessions. Not with his mother!

[JW: *This case is a good example of what often happens when a therapist is working with a child or adolescent. A good portion of this case was devoted to (a) getting a clear picture of the situation in Joey's home and (b) helping him try to develop a better plan for dealing with this annoying situation. Dr. Ellis gives him several ideas that might eliminate the problem, such as getting rid of one or more of the animals. As is often the case, the client has reasons why these alternatives will not work. I like to call these responses, "Yes, but . . . " rejoinders.*

Dr. Ellis then attempts to help the client see that he is making the problem worse by his demandingness and his tendency to "awfulize" about the animals in his home. Near the end of the session, Dr. Ellis again tries to help the client think of alternative solutions, such as the possibility of a fence. As this session illustrates, sometimes the focus needs to be on helping the client problem-solve.]

[AE: *Jerry Wilde is right. With both children and adults, REBT tries to help clients change what they can change and, as Reinhold Niebuhr said, to accept (but not like) Adversities that they cannot change. Usually, clients are making themselves so needlessly anxious, depressed, and enraged about the main Adversities of their lives, that the REBT practitioner first tries to show them how to minimize their disturbances and then to work at devising practical solutions to these adversities.*

By changing their disturbing feelings, as I tried to show Joey, they are more likely to effectively change what they can change. But REBT also, as they become less disturbed, tries to help them do considerable problem-solving so that they are afflicted with fewer Adversities. As Alfred Korzybski (1933/1990) recommended, REBT tries to handle both unfortunate A's (Adversities) that people encounter and their C's (emotional and behavioral Consequences) that they construct about their Adversities. It is therefore a comprehensive *and* integrative *system of psychotherapy (Ellis, 2001a, 2001b.].*

References

Ellis, A. (2001a). *Feeling better, getting better, and staying better.* Atascadero, CA. Impact Publishers.

Ellis, A. (2001b). *Overcoming destructive beliefs, feelings, and behaviors.* Amherst, NY: Prometheus Books.

Korzybski, A. (1933/1990). *Science and sanity.* Concord, CA: International Society for General Semantics.

A 16-Year-Old Girl
With Weight Problems

Therapist: Rod Martel

Traditional therapeutic models tend to dichotomize therapy into the *assessment* and *therapy/intervention* phases. The following transcript of an initial session with "Beverly," a female adolescent with weight issues, demonstrates the hypothetico-deductive "evolving" assessment strategy in which assessment, teaching, and therapy are intertwined in a multilevel dynamic "power" session.

Using the "session" as a stimulus, copious amounts of data are obtained about the client's family of origin, life events, medical and social history, epistemology and, most important, how her self-defeating "irrational" beliefs exacerbate her negative (and dysfunctional) emotional states.

In this model of assessment, using current and immediately available session data, the therapist actively constructs impromptu probing questions for the purpose of clarifying client belief systems and to ascertain whether or not more testing might, in fact, be warranted.

Readers of this transcript will want to try to identify the following components: assessment of irrational beliefs, tenacity/durability of irrational beliefs, disputation of irrational beliefs, relevant family history, beliefs *about* family history, reality testing, accuracy of client information, client education about rational/irrational beliefs, and agreement of therapeutic goals.

The therapist's hypothesis that the client's perfectionistic thinking, misinformation about weight, self-downing, low frustration tolerance, sense of awfulness about family abandonment, and her behaviors relating to eating disorders are all associated with her Irrational Belief system is *confirmed* in this initial session.

In contrast, the therapist's hypothesis that the client is being sexually abused, or about the extent or presence of compulsive overeating, is neither confirmed nor *dis*confirmed in this session. Also unconfirmed is the hypothesis that a genetically-based mood disorder may be present, requiring a medication evaluation and whether or not her admission of "throwing up" is isolated or habitual.

The session ends on an upbeat note after the therapist has gleaned a wealth of assessment information about everything from belief systems and family history to the often elusive adolescent admission of purging.

THERAPIST: Okay, if you had to pick one thing that really was a hassle that caused you the most pain and messed up your life the most this year, what do you think that would be?

CLIENT: My weight. It causes problems emotionally and at school.

T: How does it cause problems at school?

C: Because I always get teased and I feel uncomfortable. I'm just paranoid to be there.

T: Did you put more weight on than last year or . . .

C: It's pretty much the same but it's just, mmmmm. . . .

T: So it causes problems because you get teased at school and you don't like getting teased at school . . .

C: No! Well, last year . . . the beginning of ninth grade I was really skinny, I had slendered down a lot and I looked really good because I had got out of treatment then. And then I started getting upset being around my friends and then being at home because it was different than in there. I can do anything I want at home but I couldn't there. I feel that I'm more independent here than I was there. It's really weird and so . . . the 'frigerator was right there and nothing would happen to me if I got into it, but I just feel guilty getting into the 'frigerator.

T: This is at *your* house now?

C: My house.

T: How come you gained weight? What is the reason?

C: Mostly I was bored. I didn't do enough. I just sat home and watched TV.

T: How do people get fat?

C: Not doing enough exercise. That is what I don't do.

T: How do you feel about yourself right now about gaining all that weight?

C: It really upsets me. When I lost that weight, I had a lot more boyfriends than I do now. And it is really emotionally bad because my grandparents want me to lose weight and stuff.

T: Were you ever skinny?

C: Skinny?

T: Thin. What you call thin. Were you ever thin?

C: That was when I was pretty slender. I only would've had to lose 20 pounds and I would have been perfect. But I gained it all back.

T: I've got a whole book here about research on weight control. It's one of my favorite issues and I've done a lot of reading on it. It seems that people are born with certain tendencies to stay thin or get fat.

C: Get fat is mine.

T: Okay, and that there are certain things you can do to influence that weight one way or the other. But for the most part, if you are born with that tendency to stay thin, you're going to stay thin no matter how much you eat. Have you ever met people who eat and eat all the time and they never gain weight?

C: Yes.

T: What do you think about people like that?

C: I get mad because they always say, "I'm so fat," and they are so skinny and I go "God, you're skinny. Look at me, I'm fat," and she goes "No you're not, no you're not."

T: Have you ever seen people who are heavier—I'm not saying obese, but let's say heavy—and maybe even obese but heavier than what you consider normal, who eat not as much as other people?

C: Yeah. They have something wrong with their . . . umm, I can't remember.

T: Metabolism?

C: Yeah. I have a high metabolism.

T: Do you think there may in fact be some truth in that whole idea that people are in fact born with a tendency to be heavy or thin?

C: . . . but see I was born chubby but I was really tall, I have always been tall. My mom was skinny as a student when she was in school but then she started gaining weight after I was born. My dad has always been big and my grandma . . . it runs in my whole family altogether.

T: Okay. It runs in your family. For example, I met someone the other day where there was a genetic disease that ran in their family. I forgot what was it was called, but it was a disease where nerve endings started deteriorating and they would start losing control of a lot of their functions and this ran in the family.

C: Not mine, 'cause I can remember.

T: Right. I'm not talking about that . . . what I am saying is that there are problems that are genetic. You just mentioned to me that this runs in your family and that it is almost in the genes. We can influence that somewhat. For example, I am 5 feet 7 inches, barely. Okay? I wish that I were 5 feet 9 inches or 5 feet 10 inches. It would be easier for me to buy clothes and there would be some practical advantages, because people treat you better when you are taller, I think. I've wished that a lot of times, but is there anything I can do about that?

C: No.

T: With weight . . .

C: You *can* do some things about it.

T: Some things you can do about it. Some things you can't.

C: I know there's things I can do that would help me, that is pretty much cutting down, but most times I cut down but then I skip meals. Most times I don't even eat breakfast. I just wait until usually my dad gets home and then have something.

T: Okay. Well, Beverly, it's really tough to lose weight. I've talked to a lot of people. When you have a tendency to be overweight, it is very, very difficult. I can tell you that some of the diets that they have been doing in hospitals have been successful getting the weight off, but people put the weight back on, fast. There are some physiological reasons for that, but I don't want to get into that at this time. Let's assume that you're not going to be able to do as much about your weight as you would like to do. You may be able to do some things to get it down a little bit, and you may able to get in better shape, but let's assume for the most part that you will be a fat person. Let's just pretend that's the way it is going to be. Okay? What do you think about that?

C: I don't want to be fat all my life, because I know I'll probably die early like my mom did and I don't want to do that. I want to live.

T: What if I told you that there are some things you can do about it, but you are not going to get skinny.

C: I don't want to be skinny, I just want to be slimmer than I am now. Enough so that I can tell.

T: And there are some things you can do, and it is going to take a lot of hard work. Let's assume that you don't want to put in the hard work for the rest of your life, because it *takes* the rest of your life.

C: Then you won't get it done.

T: Okay. Can you live with yourself if you don't get it done?

C: Sometimes you feel like . . . I don't want to go through this anymore. I mean if I was fat all my life I couldn't stand it. I'd have to do something to . . . if . . . a choice you have to make between life and death. If you want to be fat then you can be fat, but that you are killing yourself there. Even by eating as much as you can, you are killing yourself, like my mom, she had all kinds of things wrong with her from eating too much.

T: By the way . . . there has never been a study done that shows that overweight people eat more than thin people do—*as a group*—I am saying. There has never been a study done that shows that overweight people eat more as a group than thin people do. You'll find lots of thin people eating a lot of food, and you will find lots of fat people eating a lot of food, and lots of fat people eating a little food, and you will find lots of skinny people eating a little food. I am saying that, as a group, the whole stereotype of fat people eating a lot of extra food is not true. The research doesn't show that. *You* may be overeating. But I am talking as a group that's not true. Now let's get back to the fact that you tend to be born with a certain tendency to be born fat or thin. Now if you were born with one leg, could you change that?

C: Yes.

T: How?

C: You could get an artificial leg.

T: But could you get a regular leg?

C: No.

T: If you were born with diabetes, could you change that?

C: No.

T: If you were born with some other ailment like . . .

C: Blindness?

T: Blindness, yes, could you change that, for the most part?

C: No.

T: No, they *stay* blind. If you were born with the *tendency* to be fat, could you change that?

C: Yeah.

T: How could you change that?

C: By doing some things about it. By not eating as much, by doing more exercise and pushing yourself.

T: . . . you can change your weight somewhat, but the research shows that you can't change your tendency to be fat. If you are born with that genetic make-up to put weight on, you are always going to have that tendency. How does a blind person survive, knowing that they are going to be blind and that they can't do anything about it?

C: They think, well . . . most of them have better hearing. They're blind but their other senses are more excellent. If they don't have one, then they get better at the other.

T: They compensate?

C: Yes.

T: How does a person who is born with one leg survive life?

C: They have to admit to themselves that they don't have another limb and so they have to do their best with what they have right now.

T: Good! Do they have to feel guilty about not having a leg?

C: No. They can feel like anybody else.

T: Does a blind person have to feel guilty about not having eyes like everybody else?

C: No. It's not their fault.

T: Do you have to feel guilty about being fat?

C: Yes!

T: Why?

C: Because you did it. Most people have done it to make themselves feel guilty. I always feel guilty.

T: Now, I thought we just discussed this whole idea that you are born with this tendency to get fat much like someone who is born with a disability like blindness, or having one leg or diabetes or something else like that. Do you believe me when I tell you that that is what the research shows—that we are born with a tendency to be thin or fat?

C: Yeah. But see I know I can be skinny because I was . . . then and I knew I could do more but then I messed up again and my tendency is to mess up.

T: Okay. Let's assume that that is the case . . . that you tried very hard and you didn't succeed; you messed up; you overate and you got fat because of your overeating. I'm not buying into that necessarily. I'm just going along with you because *you* say that is what happened. I think there are some other biological things that happened besides just the overeating because *I* can overeat and it doesn't happen.

C: Because some people have another thing that is wrong with their metabolism. It's the kind of disease where they can't lose weight. I can't remember what it is called. They can't lose weight because something is wrong with it.

T: Let's assume that you did overeat and that you lost control. You say you feel guilty about that. Now what is it about overeating that would make you feel guilty?

C: Eating more than you know that you should.

T: Okay. You ate more than you should, but why should you feel guilty about it?

C: Because you put it on.

T: You put more weight on, but why do you have to . . . why *must* you feel guilty?

C: Well, if you want to lose weight, and you know you gained it and that you didn't put enough force to do it.

T: Okay. So you didn't work as hard as you should have.

C: That you wanted to . . .

T: Now that's a reason why you *are* feeling guilty . . . why you have chosen to make yourself feel guilty, and why do you *have* to feel guilty?

C: (laughs) You don't have to but I do.

T: So you choose to make yourself feel guilty in that circumstance?

C: Yeah.

T: And do you think that is something you may want to work on yourself in the future? Not just the weight, but the *idea* that maybe you can lose your weight without making yourself feel guilty. Would that be a goal of yours?

C: Yeah.

T: Do you think you might want to do something like that . . . to lose weight *without* feeling guilty?

C: Yeah. It would make my life a lot easier. (laughs)

T: So, the guilt may not be as useful as you think, is what I am saying and you may not *have* to make yourself feel guilty. People mess up all the time because we are humans. I know I do. I mess up with my children. Sometimes I mess up in school. Sometimes I say things I wish I hadn't said to people. We mess up all the time, and sometimes I don't have as much control over my life as I would like, and *sometimes* I overeat. You know, sometimes most people overeat and lots of people that I talk to go on binges quite a bit of the time.

C: You have to have ice cream.

T: Once a week people load up and they just pig out . . .

C: (laughs)

T: Pretty common thing.

C: And a lot of people, they get real upset with themselves and they just throw it up. I've done that a few times.

T: What I am trying to get at is: Do you need to make yourself feel bad in those circumstances? You give yourself a double whammy. You've got your weight problem and then what else are you doing to yourself?

C: Making yourself feel guilty.

T: Right.

C: Making me want to eat more, too.

T: When you are spending energy on yourself to feel guilty, that is less energy to do what?

C: Lose weight.

T: Lose weight . . . to work on the *problem*. There are things you can do to help yourself feel less guilty. But mainly, because we don't have a lot of time right now, is when you are getting those feelings, ask yourself why you *have* to feel guilty? What are the reasons you have to feel guilty . . . not the reasons you *are,* but why you *must* make yourself feel that way. Because after all, aren't you a human? Aren't you a member of the human race? Don't you make mistakes?

C: Yes. (laughs)

T: Do you know people who don't make mistakes?

C: I did.

T: They *never* make mistakes? Ever?

C: Except once and that is what killed him.

[*JW: While this discussion quickly changed focus, it might have been a good idea to spend some additional time clarifying the concept. The client still might believe that some people are perfect.*]

T: So you will admit that most people screw up once in awhile?

C: Most people try to cover up so nobody can see. My grandfather did.

T: So they screw up once in awhile. Are you entitled to screw up once in awhile?

C: Yeah.

T: Does that help you feel a little bit better relative to your weight problem? You are still overweight. How do you feel if you can leave the rest of that stuff behind . . . the guilt?

C: I'd probably feel a lot better.

T: Do you think you can work on the problem better?

C: Yeah.

T: A lot of people foolishly believe they need that guilt to get things done.

C: Because it makes them more uppity to go.

T: You mentioned something about your grandfather just now. Can you tell me what has happened in the last year with your family situation? What is the most important thing in the last year?

C: My grandparents dying in the house. My grandpa and grandmother just came home after a funeral of one of their friends at church and he had put the car in the townhouse garage and he had shut the garage door. He was probably going to come back down and work on the car or something, and he left it running and he walked my grandma upstairs because she has a hard time getting up the stairs. He closed the door and walked upstairs and the noise—you couldn't hear it because it was muffled because of the concrete and stuff. He was in the bathroom washing up and grandma was making something for dinner and she had stuff in the microwave and she walked—she sat in the living room and watched TV and all of a sudden she just collapsed and my grandfather just fell to the ground in the bathroom. It was Saturday night and the next morning they were supposed to pick up some people for church, and so they didn't answer the phone or anything and a couple people stopped by and they acted like nobody was home so the lady that hadn't heard from them called my aunt and my aunt called my uncle and stuff, and they called the police and they broke in there and they found my grandma and grandpa laying there dead.

T: And where were you at that time?

C: I was in California.

T: What were you doing there?

C: Visiting my aunt and my cousins.

T: And that was how long ago that they died?

C: March 9th.

T: A few months ago. How are you doing emotionally? Is this a problem for you still? Is it interfering in your life today?

C: Not really. When they died I didn't really . . . I was sleeping when my brother had called on Monday morning. Sunday he tried getting ahold of us but we were at Disneyland and Monday morning early he called and he told my dad that . . . I was sleeping on the couch and the kitchen is right there by it, and all of a sudden I heard "My in-laws died!" And then my cousin was saying "carbon monoxide." I woke up and walked in there and started crying and said "No!" I didn't believe him. I just thought he said that just to get us home or something.

T: It sounds like it was a really traumatic thing but it's not something that is interfering in your life every day right now.

C: Not yet. I still haven't felt as much as I should . . . well, it's not . . . it's like . . . see I knew my grandparents better than my mom because my mom was never there.

T: Could you say that again? I didn't hear the last sentence.

C: My mom was never around me. She never really took care of me when I was little, and my grandparents, me and them got along but my grandpa was perfect. I mean he sure covered up a lot to make sure that he didn't. He always acted like he was "Mr. Hotshot" 'cause he knew everything, 'cause he knew he didn't have no problems in the world.

T: But you got along with your grandmother pretty well.

C: Yeah.

T: Where was your mom when you were growing up?

C: She was running around. She was in and out of treatment centers for five . . . God . . . since I was about eight years old until I was thirteen and a half, she died.

T: Now do you know what she was in the treatment center for?

C: She was manic depressive and she would have sprees and she would go out all night and go to Perkins® and stay all night there and then one time she called and see I hadn't seen her all day and I go "Where are you?" and I said "When are you coming home?" and she said "Well, let me talk to dad" and I said "Dad's outside" and she goes "Why don't you guys take the truck and come down here?" And I said "Why should we go down there?" and this was, God . . . about seven or eight and I said "No, why don't you come home? Don't you care about me?" She was never there. One time she brought a couple over to our house and they stayed over at our house a couple of times, and it caused a lot of traumatic stuff in my house because I was close to the lady but my mom had the hots for her husband or something and they were starting an argument and stuff and . . .

T: It sounds like you had a tough time . . . your mom died when you were how old?

C: Thirteen and a half.

T: Your dad has been taking care of you ever since.

C: Before that! She was looking at all the other kids . . . "Oh they're so cute!" She would like other kids but not us. At times she took care of us and stuff, but she was having a lot of problems herself because she wasn't grown up herself. My grandpa and grandma let her off by not doing things and stuff. When my grandpa was living, my grandpa always spoiled us. That was my dad's dad . . . he was not like my mom at all because she was a lazy bum.

T: Do you miss your mother?

C: Somewhat. Not really, because she was never really there.

T: How do you get along with your father now?

C: Me and him are real close. We have always been close but I'm trying to get more away because when I look at guys he always says "Is that all you think about . . . boys?" and I say "Yeah . . . so do you always think about girls and looking at their butt and all that stuff . . . Why can't a girl do that? It's natural you know?" And when I have boyfriends and kiss and stuff he would just get "Well, as soon as you start kissing, it always leads to sex." I said "It don't always."

T: When you have problems with your father, what kind of problems are they?

C: Overprotective.

T: What does he do?

C: He doesn't want me to go out. Sometimes he doesn't want me to go out so he makes me feel sad so I stay home with him and keep him company. I've always had a problem with that.

T: Do you do that? Do you stay home with him?

C: Usually I'm in the other room 'cause I can't stand sitting in the kitchen 'cause if I sit in the kitchen I'll be grabbing something out of the refrigerator.

T: So how often does that happen where you feel like he makes you feel guilty and then you stay home instead of going out?

C: Well, tonight a friend of mine called and asked to go see a movie with me and my dad said, "Well, doesn't it seem like she is trying to get you or something 'cause you never talk to her on the phone." And he will just say, "Well, maybe she is just setting up something?" but I'm not going anyway because I have to go and babysit.

T: So in this case, he didn't really make you feel guilty, you just decided to go babysit.

C: Well, I just found out today that I was going to babysit. I was planning on going but then decided not to . . .

T: But there are times when you stay home because you don't want to leave him by himself?

C: Yeah because he has threatened before that he would leave me and never come back . . .

T: If what?

C: If I didn't shape up. He thinks that . . . he just makes me really upset sometimes because he's drinking a lot. A lot of times I could fall back on my grandpa or grandma . . . I went over there and one time I said I never wanted to come back home. I never ran away but I was tempted.

T: It must be rough over there for you sometimes. It sounds like you have had to become more grown up than . . .

C: I have had to . . . I've had to grow up fast since I was about eight or something. I had to take care of myself most of the time. Well, my dad was there but my dad had had a bad time with my brother and when we are driving, he always makes me so nervous. My dad is having a hard time with my brother and when we are driving he always makes me so nervous that I do wrong things. A lot of times when he is drunk, he yells, "God damn! You . . . bitch!" and stuff. And I just say I'm not wrong and I'm not no whore either, just because I go out with guys and stuff. He says "As soon as you get knocked up, you are getting out of this house . . . I'll kick you out!" And I say, "Yeah, I'm sure I'm going to go and get pregnant."

T: It sounds like you have a tough situation right now. The trick is to be able to live there as best as you can right now. What are your other options?

C: Nothing. I mean I think I would be a lot better if I moved to California, because I can be with my cousin and stuff, but he says, "Yeah, you'll probably be laying around in the desert and stuff." As soon as I'm 18 I'm moving to L.A.

T: Does your father love you, as far as you know?

C: Yeah.

T: How do you know?

C: Affection . . . you know, I get hugs and stuff. He always says that he loves me and stuff and that he is doing it because he thinks it helps me. I said it doesn't help me at all, it just makes me feel more hurt.

T: Are most people made up of good things and bad things?

C: Yeah.

T: Or all good things?

C: No.

T: Or all bad things?

C: In between. (laughs)

T: Is he on one side or the other, or is he in the middle?

C: Little over to the bad because . . .

T: So he has lots of good things and a lot of bad things.

C: His drinking for one thing. His bitching all the time. God, [my brother] moved out because he couldn't stand it and stuff. He always gets mad at me because . . . see my cat just had kittens yesterday and I would like to go look at them and he says "God, you always have to go bother that poor cat! If she kills those cats, I'm going to kick you out of the house!" And I mean, I'm sure, I'm petting it . . . and that's my cat and stuff. He just yells . . . sometimes he just bellers and stuff.

T: Tell me about your friends? Do you have any close friends?

C: I did. We're not close any more because my dad couldn't stand her.

T: What happened?

C: He called her a slut.

T: Now who called who what?

C: My dad called her a slut.

T: Why isn't she *your* friend? That's what your *dad* said but why isn't she *your* friend?

C: Her mom don't want her to have nothing to do with me. She said I'm in a dream world and I'm not doing anything about my weight, I don't do nothing at all. She is mental! She is crazy. She makes the kids do everything in the house. She's got a mentally retarded sister, and she's a pain in the ummm!

T: So she's not your friend anymore. Do you have any friends now?

C: Yeah. I could go to friends' houses but sometimes I just say naah.

T: Why don't you go?

C: Sometimes I feel uncomfortable. I feel insecure being around people.

T: Why is that?

C: My weight. Most of the time I just don't want people to see me. Almost everybody I see that I have never seen before [says] "You are so beautiful . . . if you just got down on your weight, you would be just perfect!" And I go "Oh, God!"

T: You get tired of hearing that . . .

C: Yes, and plus I want to be a model. Well, see, right now we don't have the money, but I want to be a model some day because I think I would be a good one but . . .

T: Every time we start talking we end up back on your weight.

C: Because a lot of my problems just surround about my weight. Sometimes I don't like being around my friends because I mean most of them are partiers and all they want to do is drink and I don't like that because I am not an alcoholic or anything. I like to go to parties but not necessarily to drink but to meet guys.

T: What is the worst thing that could happen if you stayed at the present weight that you are right now and you went out and you went to a party; what is going to happen that you fear so much?

C: They would pick on me or start talking about me . . . mostly behind my back. I always can tell when people are talking about me. I get really paranoid 'cause I think people are talking about me but they aren't. I'm used to it.

T: Let's assume that they *are* talking about you . . . let's assume they are saying that you are fat.

C: I say, "Well that's my problem and if you don't like it, that's too bad! If you don't like the way I look then that's too bad because that's the way I am right now." That does not help me at all. If they want me to lose weight and if they don't like the way I look right now, then they should help me. 'Cause I am sick of people saying, "Yeah look at her . . . monster, ain't she?"

T: Are you the same as your weight? Is B. the same as how many pounds she is? Is that who you are? Does it describe you as a person . . . totally?

C: No.

T: Why not?

C: Because, I mean you have personality and, you know, a sense of humor and everything like that and stuff, but people are like . . . but most guys are really out for one thing . . . messing around and stuff and they just look on the outside and they say that, "She does have a pretty face but she is so fat."

T: But that is possibly true . . . I can't argue that point.

C: I *know* it is true!

T: But are *you* the same as your weight? Do you still have redeeming and good qualities even though you may be overweight?

C: People just don't look at it that way . . . they just think "Oh, God."

T: What is important right now is how *you* look at it.

C: Sometimes I stick up for my rights and sometimes I just let it go and it just makes me feel worse.

T: What makes you feel bad about it?

C: I don't stick up for myself. People go on talking about me and both my grandparents say, "Well, just don't say nothing," but it doesn't help at all because it just keeps on digging at me. Nobody knows more than me 'cause I have felt it since I was in kindergarten.

T: What kinds of things did they say about you?

C: They would call me "bitch" and stuff like that and they would . . .

T: *Are* you a bitch?

C: No. I don't think I am a bitch.

T: If I say you are green, does that make you green?

C: (laughing) No.

T: So how does calling you a "bitch" make you a bitch?

C: I don't necessarily believe everything they say I am but . . .

T: Well, then why are you getting so mad about it? It sounds to me that if you didn't believe part of it, you wouldn't get so mad about it.

C: Well, I know I'm big, I know I'm fat. It's really weird, because people make me so mad. Sometimes I just want to scream and start whipping people's butts and smack! Leave me alone . . . God! That's why I don't want to go out anymore 'cause I'm afraid that they might make me feel hurt and stuff, because I'm sick of being hurt. I've been hurt more than most people have in their life. It's really getting me tired.

T: Did you ever hear that saying "sticks and stones can break my bones but . . . "

C: Yes, and it's bull!

T: You don't believe that one.

C: 'Cause it *does* hurt. I know some people who are really rough and tough and they say, "You say something about me and I'll kick your living mmm . . . "

T: Let's assume that people are going to call you names for the rest of your life and that you are not going to lose the weight. Let's assume that that's the case because that may happen. Maybe it won't, maybe it will. If people call you names and you stay heavier for the rest of your life, what can we do about it then?

C: You can't really do anything.

T: Are you going to get upset each and every time someone calls you a name?

C: Not every time.

T: Do you believe you have control over your own life, your own emotions? Do you believe in that? Would that not be a goal for you to work on . . . to get control over how you feel and get control over your own emotions? Would you like it if people could call you names and you wouldn't be happy about it, but you wouldn't be so angry that you wanted to kill them? I'm not saying you are going to be happy about it. We call that developing a thick skin. (client chuckles)

C: But see it's kind of hard when you've been . . . I mean . . . being teased as long as I have, you should get used to it but, I mean, I thought people would be different . . . more nicer to persons. Its just like prejudice against black people or Chinese or Indians. We always pick on them but what about them picking on us?

T: Do people in this world pick on other people?

C: Yeah. A lot.

T: Isn't that the way the world is?

C: It is, but it shouldn't be.

T: Well, *isn't* that reality? Are people stupid in this world?

C: Yes.

T: Do they act foolishly?

C: Yes.

T: Are they ignorant?

C: Yes.

T: Are they biased?

C: Yes.

T: So isn't that the way the world is?

C: Yes.

T: Is ranting and raving and getting angry and kicking and screaming going to change the world?

C: (laughing) Depends.

[*JW: I would have asked Beverly to explain what she means by "depends." Rod has done a very nice job of pointing out that some people act in ignorant and biased ways and that simply* demanding *it not be so will not impact reality. I would have spent a little more time making sure Beverly understood that point. I've had this discussion with a lot of adolescents and it's not uncommon for clients to agree to this point, but down deep they still feel like "it shouldn't be."*]

T: Well, you sure have a hell of a lot of anger and resentment and you told me you feel guilty and has that changed the people you deal with? Do they still talk behind your back?

C: Yes. Most of them do but if I find out about them, they know I'll be really mad. Because I have a look and when people see that, they never come by me until they see that I've calmed down. My friends had noticed that because I get really mad easily. My friend is a dumb ding-dong; she is a total dork.

T: How come?

C: Because she goes "ahhhhhh!" (high-pitched squeal). She has a weird laugh and she drives me crazy.

T: You told me you weren't close to anybody.

C: Well, she is my friend, but I don't talk to her very much. But there is Pam because me and her are pretty close because I've known her all my life. We are just really good friends and she don't care what I look like. She always says "Oh Beverly, you're not fat." She is a mouse. She is really skinny.

T: I didn't tell you you weren't fat, did I? I don't believe in lying to people, and you are heavier than the average person. What I asked was, "Why do you have to condemn yourself because of it?"

C: Because that's the way other people think that it is and that I think, too.

T: Why do you have to think that way? Give me some reasons.

C: Looking in the mirror!

T: It's true, you are heavier than most people but why do you have to down yourself and say Beverly is a terrible, lousy person because of it?

C: That's the way I am treated.

T: It's true. People treat you badly. Why do you have to treat yourself badly?

C: I don't know, but I do.

T: That's the question you can keep asking yourself. Why do you need to give yourself a double whammy? Let me know if you come up with a good reason for that because most people can't prove why they have to down themselves as a human.

C: I already feel worse, so what is the difference?

T: You told me a lot of good things about yourself, too. Maybe you could accentuate those a little bit?

C: People . . . they never really think about how other people feel just as long as they can say something and *then* they feel really guilty for it . . . most people do.

T: But that's other people. People are going to act the way they act. I'm talking about *you* getting control over how *you* feel about yourself.

C: I think the only way I could cure that is if I lose more weight and I feel better about myself.

T: What if you never lose weight? Are you going to feel lousy your whole life?

C: True. (laughs)

T: Are there any fat people in the whole world who might not down themselves as a human and might feel okay about themselves?

C: Yeah.

T: How do they do that?

C: I don't know? (laughs)

T: Would you like to learn it?

C: They don't look at themselves.

T: Let's assume that they *do* look at themselves.

C: They say "Oh, what the hell." I can't do that with myself because I don't feel comfortable with myself. I feel insecure.

T: You haven't done it up to *now*. It doesn't mean you can't do it in the *future*. It takes hard work . . . a lot of work to do that. Would you like to learn how?

C: Sure.

[*JW: That final "sure" often has the unexpressed meaning, "Sure I would like to learn how, but I want it to be easy." Low Frustration Tolerance is such a common component of behavioral and emotional problems and is often found in clients with weight-control difficulties. It's a good idea to assume low frustration tolerance is present and do some probing for the beliefs often associated with it, such as "It will take too long. I've tried that before and it didn't work. I can't stand depriving myself."*]

[*AE: This client sticks stubbornly to the irrational belief, "I'm too fat, as I must not be, and my* fatness *makes me an inadequate and unlovable* person. *Rod Martell tries several rational ways of disputing these ideas, but makes little inroads into them.*

1. The therapist shows the client that she may well have a genetic disposition to easily gain and regain weight. So he indicates to her that she is by no means totally responsible for her fatness. This is a legitimate disposition but is somewhat inelegant, and she does not buy it and exonerate herself.

2. The therapist tries to show the client that even if she is somewhat responsible for being overweight, she need not be guilty or self-deprecating for being so. He indicates that, like all humans, she is quite fallible and can accept herself as fallible. That is a good argument—but, again, the client acknowledges her fallibility without giving up her guilt. Rod Martell also shows her that her guilt and self-denigration won't help her lose weight and instead make her side-track and waste time and energy instead of devoting it to weight reduction. This is also a good point, but the client gets involved in relating her grandfather's and grandmother's accidental death by asphyxiation and never quite sees how self-defeating her guilt is.

3. The client also relates how her mother, who was manic-depressive, was critical and demanding, and how her father, who is an alcoholic, is also overly critical. But before the therapist can work on her not taking her parents neglect and criticism too seriously and seemingly putting herself down, she gets back to her main problem—castigating herself for being overweight.

4. The therapist forthrightly uses REBT to tackle the client's self-downing for her weight and for other people's disapproval. He valiantly tries to help her achieve unconditional self-acceptance. At times, he says, her behavior *may be bad but that never makes her a bad* person. *She says that people are unfairly prejudiced against her for her fatness. He makes the telling point that if they unfairly berate her, she doesn't also have to treat* herself *badly. That produces a double whammy for her! Once again she resists seeing this important point.*

Although the therapist makes some excellent points, the client only sees them lightly and still firmly hangs on to her abysmal self-deprecation. It will probably take many more REBT sessions to help her achieve unconditional self-acceptance. I suspect that she may have a severe personality disorder, such as endogenous depression, that has both biological and environmental roots. Just as her disposition to easily gain weight is, as the therapist notes, partly genetic, so too may be her strong tendency to defame herself. Rod Martell is on the right track to help her achieve unconditional self-acceptance, but it may take some time for her to do so.]

[*JW: This case is a nice example of what I like to call "switching the* A." *The client keeps bringing up new Activating events whenever Rod Martell starts to help her critically examine her thinking and her responsibility (ownership) in this problem. She brings up her grandparents' accidental deaths as the therapist is starting to dispute some of her irrational thinking, and later in the session switches the* A *to her parents. I don't believe this is an intentional attempt by the client to avoid owning some of the responsibility. It is usually a sign the therapist is getting "too close for comfort." It can be very scary for clients to accept the fact that they are at least partially responsible for their circumstances. It is always much safer and easier to blame parents, friends, or the whole of society. Unfortunately, clients do* not *have the power to control other people, nor do they have the ability to go back in time and relive earlier experiences. That is why helping them accept their role in their circumstances* and *their ability to change their thinking is so important. To a certain extent, their thinking and behavior might be the only things they can control.*]

6 | A 10-Year-Old Boy With Anger Problems

Therapist: Jerry Wilde, Ph.D.

This chapter contains transcriptions of three sessions with a fourth-grade boy who was 10 years old. He was referred to an anger control group I was conducting but, due to the limited number of spaces, "John" was not included in the group.

John has been a concern to his forth-grade teacher due to his problem with anger but also because of his tendency to create rather elaborate lies. The fabrications were what I like to call "crazy lies." Some lies have an obvious intention such as avoiding punishment. This type of lying, although still a concern, at least makes some sort of sense. Crazy lying is the type of lying that does not appear to have a purpose other than to impress others.

John had the type of anger problem that was not a daily concern. He would hold his anger in until he exploded in a fit of rage. When this occurred, he usually was under some type of stress at home. John was a likeable young man and seemed to pick up on the REBT concepts quickly.

SESSION ONE

THERAPIST: When we were walking down here you said you got in trouble and then I asked you a little bit about what happened there. So go ahead and start back with what you were saying.

Reprinted from *Anger management in schools: alternatives to student violence,* transcriptions, with permission from Technomic Publishing Company, Lancaster, PA.

CLIENT: Okay. I went to the bathroom but they were being too loud. Chris pushed me into the door, I mean into that thing that you . . .

T: Paper towel?

C: Yeah, and I hit my head and I almost got in trouble for that. But see, you're not allowed to go in the bathroom . . . or, if it's too loud you have to get out.

T: Okay.

C: And, see, I went in it and I was trying to get out and Chris just goes, "Your mother is fat," and all that, and Mrs. Townsend heard and . . . .

T: So you almost got in trouble for that.

C: And I go, I had to talk to Mrs. Swenson (the principal), and Mrs. Smith (his teacher) said, "Why don't you just let them go because I think they learned a lesson." That was me and Billy, Chris, and Tim and. . . .

T: So you didn't get in trouble but you almost did. You were saying that . . . What teacher did you almost get in trouble with? Mr. Black?

It became clear that this story was not leading anywhere so I interrupted and tried to move the discussion to another topic. One of the advantages of REBT is that it is very problem focused and does not promote the notion that the therapist must listen to endless stories from the client. REBT practitioners are free to be very active with the client and direct the session where they feel it had better go.

C: No, Smith.

T: Oh, but there was a different time. Not in the bathroom.

C: Uhm . . . what time was it?

T: That you might have to serve a detention.

C: That was Mrs. Swenson.

T: Mrs. Swenson . . . Okay.

C: And she said to me and Tim, because Chris had said, "Stay away from me," and he hit Billy with a baseball bat and Billy hit him back.

T: So you guys all got sent to the office.

C: Yeah, we all had to go talk to Mrs. Swenson. And she said me and Billy could go back to class, 'cause she thought we learned our lesson. And we did.

T: Good.

C: Tim got an after-school detention.

I never did quite understand what went on with the baseball bat, paper towel holder, etc., but John was not bothered by what had transpired. So I moved ahead once again.

T: What I wanted to talk to you a little bit about today is how sometimes we get angry about stuff and that can lead to other kinds of problems. Now let me ask you, see if you can think back to a time when you got really angry about something. Something that happened in the last few days maybe or the last week or last month.

C: Last month when I got in trouble for my brother.

T: Okay. Tell me about that.

C: See, he was ripping up my baseball cards and the cards were really good to me (I took this to mean the cards were really important to him) and my mom said, "Stop him from doing that" and I got really angry and started calling him names.

T: Uh-huh, this is your little brother right?

C: Yeah.

T: So you got really angry. Were you more angry at your mom or at your little brother?

C: I was more angry at my little brother.

T: Yeah, because he was ripping stuff up. Were you also angry because you got in trouble and it wasn't really your fault?

C: Yeah.

T: Let me ask you about times here at school. Have you ever gotten into trouble there because you were really angry and you said something or did something that you probably shouldn't have done?

C: People were playing soccer, you know, out by the tennis courts and they were using hands.

T: They were cheating?

C: And you're not supposed to use hands and I said something inappropriate like, "Knock it off. Shut up," and all that and I got told on.

I was very surprised to have a fourth grader use the phrase "I said something inappropriate" but that was his choice of words.

T: So you didn't get in real trouble but you were angry that they weren't playing the game the right way. That's not really fair that they were using their hands and stuff. What I want to try and help explain is that people think, I bet you think, that people using their hands and cheating at this game is what made you angry.

At this point it is time to introduce the concept of the ABCs.

C: Yeah.

T: But you know what?

C: What?

T: Actually that's not quite right. It's something a little different. But that's what most people think isn't it? Let me draw something here. We're going to say here at point A what happened was people were using their hands in soccer. How about we just put down people were cheating at soccer. Down here at point C you were really angry. Okay? Now like I said, what most people think is that [what happens] at point A, people cheating at soccer, causes you to be angry at point C. Actually there is a middle part, here at point B, that happens that actually makes you angry. But let me tell you a story to see if I can help explain this. Let's pretend you and I are going to go on a trip on a bus. Where are we going to go?

C: The Ozarks.

T: The Ozarks, all right, the Ozarks on a bus. So we're riding on a bus and you're sitting in the middle and I'm by the aisle and there is somebody by the window. All of a sudden, for no reason, you get poked in the ribs. It's a real hard poke that really hurts.

C: Did he mean to poke me?

T: Let's not worry about that just now. How would you probably feel if you got poked in the ribs?

J: Mad.

T: Okay. Good and mad and probably angry, so we put that down here at C and it's the same idea that we just talked about, that people think getting poked in the ribs is what makes you angry. But now you're angry and your ribs hurt and you turn over and you look and you see that it was a blind man and he was taking off his sweater because he was hot and he accidentally poked you right in the ribs 'cause he couldn't see you. What do you think you'd feel at that point?

C: Sad.

T: Maybe sad. Why do you think you'd feel sad?

C: Because he's a blind person and he didn't mean to do it and probably felt bad for it.

T: Now you know what is really interesting is that getting poked in the ribs, that still happened, didn't it? But you feel two different ways, don't you? At first, when you thought he did it on purpose, you were mad, weren't you? But then when you saw it was a blind man you were sad, because he didn't mean to and he's blind. Now you know what that shows us? There must be a middle part, B, that changes how you feel? Do you understand me?

C: Yeah.

T: Explain it to me.

A client can say he or she understands but not be clear regarding a concept. It is always a good idea to check for understanding, especially when you are introducing important concepts.

C: There must be a middle part to make you feel two different things.

T: Right. Let's look at that a little closer. When you first got poked and were mad and angry, what could you have been thinking to yourself to make yourself angry about being poked in the ribs?

C: It was on purpose.

T: So it was on purpose

I wrote down the first part even though I know there's a second Irrational Belief that follows this initial statement. The belief "It was on purpose" is probably irrational as well because there is no proof that the poke was intentional.

> What are you saying to yourself about people poking people in the ribs on purpose? "He poked me in the ribs on purpose and . . . ."

This is an example of the "complete the sentence" technique that can help clients find that second, Irrational Belief that can exist without the client's awareness.

C: I felt bad.

T: Okay, let me see if I can help. See if you can use this word to finish the sentence. Try to use the word "should" or "shouldn't" when you finish the sentence. He poked me in the ribs on purpose and . . .

C: He shouldn't have done it.

John was like a lot of clients who, on their initial exposure to REBT, need assistance finding the Irrational Belief. The goal is to help the client get to the point where he or she can do this easily, without any outside assistance.

T: "He shouldn't have done it." That's exactly right. Let me put that down. You know what? You know why I know that word "shouldn't" is real important? Because whenever we're getting really mad and angry, do you know what is going on?

C: You shouldn't do it.

T: (laughing) What's really going on is that we're demanding that somebody act differently than they acted. Aren't we? When we say "He shouldn't have done it," aren't we kind of saying "I demand that he not do this"?

C: Yeah.

T: And you know the problem with that?

C: You're demanding something from other people and they might not agree with you.

It is rare for a 10-year-old to be able to spontaneously make a rational statement like the one John made. Don't be alarmed if your clients don't catch on as quickly. John was a good client to work with and that's why I chose to use the transcription of his session for this book.

T: That's exactly right. Who controls how this guy on the bus acts? Do we?

C: No.

T: Who does?

C: Him.

T: He does, doesn't he? And whenever we demand that other people act a certain way, it's sort of like we're pretending to be God, isn't it? Sort like we're saying, "I am God and I demand that you not do this." And like you said, we're not God and we don't control them. Now, here's the second part of this. You looked over and saw that he was a blind person, right? And you instantly thought something else. What did you probably think to make yourself feel sad or at least not be mad?

C: He was taking off his sweater and he didn't mean to hit me.

T: Didn't mean to hit me.

C: It was an accident.

T: That's right. It was an accident. And you see how once you thought, "It was an accident," your anger went away right away, didn't it? Right away you said you felt sad instead of mad. Now, let's take what we're talking about with the blind man and move it up here to people cheating on soccer. Remember, we're talking about people using their hands, which is against the rules, and you got angry and mad. What do you think you were saying to yourself about people cheating that made you angry? See if you can use that word again.

C: That they shouldn't do it because that's cheating.

T: That's right. They shouldn't do it because that's cheating. That's really good. Now you know what, how could we change this demand, this "shouldn't," to more of a wish or preference? Do you know what the word preference means? It's a big word and it sort of means if you had your choice between steak and pizza, which would you prefer?

C: Pizza.

T: Okay, you'd choose pizza. So instead of saying "I *demand* steak or I *demand* pizza," if you said "I would *prefer* to have pizza," how could we change that should or shouldn't into . . . what kind of word could we use?

C: I'd *prefer* that they wouldn't use hands in soccer.

T: (writing this down) "I'd prefer that they wouldn't use hands in soccer." Now can you see that the real difference between these two is the "shouldn't." "They shouldn't do it because that's cheating" . . . that's a commandment, isn't it? We talked about pretending we're God. But if you said, "I'd prefer that they wouldn't use their hands in soccer," or do you know another word you could use? I wish they *wouldn't*.

C: That's what I was going to say.

T: You were going to say that? Okay. I *wish* they wouldn't but they can. Do you see how that would make you a lot less angry?

C: Yeah.

T: That's really good. You picked up on that really well. But I knew you would because you're a bright young man. Now which do you prefer, soccer or baseball?

C: I prefer both.

T: Good. You know what? Whenever you find yourself getting really angry about
something, if you can stop and listen to what you are saying to yourself, I'll
almost guarantee there will be a "should" or a "must" or a "ought to" or a "have
to" or any of those. If you can stop and listen to those, you know what? You
won't be angry. If you can change those "shouldn'ts" into words like "I wish" or
"I prefer." Or another phrase might be "It would be better if people didn't cheat
in soccer but people are going to do what they are going to do." It's sort of like
it would have been better if Chris wouldn't have pushed you into the towel
holder but you or I or even Mrs. Swenson can't control what Chris does. Do you
understand that?

C: Yep.

T: What I think we ought to do is to get together next week and talk some more.
Would you like that?

C: Yeah.

T: I want you to look for situations where you might make yourself angry and try
really hard to listen for those "shoulds" and "shouldn'ts" and see if you can't
change them into "wishes." Can you try and do that?

C: Yes.

Summary of Week One

John was a motivated client and picked up on the logic of REBT quickly. As I said,
sessions don't always go this well and this one was especially enjoyable because it
was the first time he had been introduced to these ideas. I have found that to take
a solid approach to REBT, it may be best to use the following sequence of activities
for the first session:

1. Ask clients for an anger problem or a situation where they anger themselves (i.e.,
   identify and get the client to agree upon the *A*).
2. Get the client to describe the emotion or *C*.
3. Explain that *A* does not cause *C*; there is a middle part, *B*.
4. Use "the blind man on the bus" story to illustrate that *B* largely causes *C*.
5. Move the logic of "the blind man" to the problem the client presented.
6. Help the client identify the *B* that is causing his or her anger.
7. Help him or her change the Irrational Belief into a Rational Belief.
8. Give a homework assignment to practice that helps the client practice using the
   new Rational Belief.

SESSION TWO

T: Do you remember what your homework assignment was for this week?

C: No.

T: It was to try to see, we were talking about anger . . .

C: Oh, yeah, that's right.

T: Now do you remember?

C: Yeah.

T: See if you can tell me what your homework assignment was.

C: You told me to see if I could do what we talked about.

T: Right, I wanted you to try to think of a situation where you might normally have gotten angry and to keep yourself from getting angry.

C: Like I did on the soccer field.

T: Well, let me hear about it. Tell me exactly what you did.

C: Well, I didn't say . . .

T: First, tell me what happened and then tell me what you did to keep from getting angry.

C: People were saying swear words when someone would score a goal or something, and I said, "I wish you wouldn't say swears," and they just said, "Okay." Then we played and I said, "I'll tell the teacher if you say swears," but I didn't get mad.

T: Right.

C: They just said things like, "Oh, shoot."

T: So not real swears?

C: Yeah.

T: But kind of like swear words. So what did you do about that? What did you think?

C: I thought it was nice that they stopped it.

T: If they had continued to use swear words, what could you have thought to yourself to not make yourself angry?

C: I can always go tell the teacher.

T: Okay, you could have told the teacher. But what could you have thought to yourself instead of thinking, "They have to not swear" or "They shouldn't swear"? What could you have thought to yourself?

C: They shouldn't swear.

T: Okay, but if you use "shouldn't," that's still a demand and you'd probably still get angry.

C: I wish.

T: I wish they wouldn't use swear words.

C: But it's their body and it's a free country.

T: That's right. And you know who controls their mouth and their voice? They do, don't they?

C: You can't go outside and talk it over and say, "I'm going to quit this right now." See my dad smokes and he tried to quit and you know those pads that you put on your arm?

T: Yeah.

C: He went in the sun one day and it burned him. So he took it off. My mom and I wish he would quit it, because it can lead to damage, but now when he smokes he goes outside.

T: So at least he doesn't smoke in the house.

C: Well, sometimes he does. But he goes in a different area.

T: You know what really impresses me? You realize that if your dad is going to smoke, he's going to smoke. You can either really, really upset yourself about that, which isn't going to change whether or not he smokes . . .

C: My mom used to smoke but my brother coughed when she smoked. Then he would turn his nose up so my mom quit, and I was really happy. But that doesn't make my dad quit.

T: That's right. And like I was just saying, whether or not you upset yourself, is that going to make your dad quit?

C: No.

T: No, probably not.

C: My dad has tried to quit twice.

T: He's tried to, so maybe he will.

C: Have you ever seen an ashtray that can pull in the smoke?

T: Yes, I know what you mean.

C: We're trying to find one for him, so he can smoke and be in the living room.

T: And it won't go all over the house. That's a good idea. I used to see those on television. Maybe you'll see a commercial with it on.

C: My mom is trying to find one.

T: It's really good that you're thinking real clearly about this. If people want to swear on the soccer field, they're going to do that. You *wish* they wouldn't but they have the right to. It's a free country, like you said. And also what you're thinking about your dad smoking. "I wish he wouldn't. I hope he quits, but I'm not going to ruin my life worrying about this and demanding he quit." Who's the only person you can really demand anything from and expect to get something?

C: Me.

T: That's right!

C: I know I'm not going to smoke but I want to get an earring, though.

T: You want to get an earring. Do you think my earring looks good?

C: Yeah.

T: Okay.

C: I really want to get an earring but my dad won't let me.

T: Maybe when you're a little older.

C: He said if I get an earring I have to wear a dress to school.

T: (laughing) I was a lot older than you when I got an earring. I was in college.

C: My mom thinks I should be old enough to pay for my own earring. But I'm not using my college money.

T: That's probably not a good idea. My dad wasn't real happy when I got my earring either. But he got over it eventually.

C: I have enough money to go to college, and I don't want to spend it because I want to go to college so bad.

T: Well, if you really want to then you probably will.

C: You know Larry Johnson? He could have played basketball earlier, but he stayed in college. I got the card of him when he was in college and I was really happy. I want to be like that.

T: You want to go to college.

C: Yeah, I want to be in the NBA, just like Larry Johnson.

T: That sounds like a good goal to have. You know what is a good idea? To get a college degree just in case you don't make the pros. You can get a good job anyway.

C: Yeah, you can be a lawyer and get a Lamborghini. Did you know doctors can get any kind of car they want? The kind of car I want is a Lamborghini.

T: You have to make a lot of money to have one of those. You know what I'd like to know? How are you going to remember some of the lessons we learned? What are you going to do to think about those things over the summer?

C: I'll probably. . . . I'm not sure.

T: Can you remind yourself when you get angry?

C: Yeah.

T: What will you think to yourself?

C: I'll think that every time they do something I don't like, I'll try to think "I wish" instead of "he should."

T: Try to keep those "shoulds" from becoming too common and keep them to wishes and preferences.

C: Yeah.

T: That will keep you a lot calmer. You won't have the same kind of problems with getting mad. That's a good goal to have. I'll probably see you one more time before the summer vacation but if I don't, have a great summer. I'll see you for sure next fall because you'll be back and I'll be back. Let's get you back to class now because I don't want you to miss too much English.

Summary for Week Two

John had an opportunity to practice his Rational Belief (RB) on the soccer field and seemed to do a pretty good job of remaining only irritated when the other players used swear words. He wanted to spend some therapy time talking about things, such as his father's smoking and college plans, which are not directly related to the presenting problem. What I have found over the years is that young people often desire a few minutes of your time to talk about things other than the presenting problem. Although REBT is very problem-focused, this does not mean that a few minutes of a session cannot be used to hear about the client's life in other areas that are unrelated to his or her difficulty. Remember, a majority of the clients are not self-referred. John did not seek me out for help; I went to him.

There are usually opportunities to reinforce REBT concepts, even in a complaint not related to the client's central problem. Note that I tried to help John see that it wouldn't do any good to get angry about his father's smoking because his father was the person who was responsible for his smoking. Getting upset about his father's smoking wouldn't help John unless it moved him toward some therapeutic action.

WEEK THREE

T: So what have you been up to since we talked last?

C: Really nothing. I slept over at a friend's house Friday and Saturday.

T: Whose house?

C: Billy's.

T: Was that fun?

C: Yeah, he has a Nintendo.

T: I bet you played that all night.

C: Not really. We played basketball outside.

T: Now do you play soccer in the summer?

C: Yes. Do you know if they are going to have the summer rec program this summer?

T: I've heard that, but I'm not sure if that's true or not. I know there's going to be swimming. I know that for sure.

C: My mom said there was going to be basketball, baseball, and swimming. And maybe soccer and football.

T: Well, I hope they do offer all that.

C: But it's going to cost more money.

T: Yeah. That's what I've heard, too.

C: So my mom said I can only do three sports.

T: So you're only going to play your top three.

C: You know Arnold. He was the lifeguard at Booth Lake last summer and he didn't think I could swim very good, so he made me take a test. I passed it and now I can swim there whenever I want.

T: So now you can swim with everybody else?

C: Yeah, I can swim way out.

T: Good.

C: They thought I was too little.

T: Then you had to pass the test where you swim around the buoys for them.

C: Yeah.

T: Good.

C: Except I sort of cheated because the sand was so close to me when I was swimming that I kept on touching it so I kept on going.

I tried to spend a short amount of time at the beginning of this session catching up on John's activities since our last visit.

T: You know what? What I wanted to talk about was what we talked about last time. About ways that we make ourselves angry. Can you tell me a little bit about what you remember that we talked about?

C: People cheating.

T: Right. People cheating at soccer, and things like that. You were saying that when people use their hands and cheat and things like that, you get angry. What I'm wondering is, can you remember what you say to yourself to make yourself angry?

C: What was the question again?

T: Do you remember what you say to yourself to make yourself really angry? Do you remember that key word "should" or "shouldn't"?

C: They shouldn't do it, because that's cheating.

T: Yeah. Remember how we talked about that's kind of a demand that people *should* do this or they *shouldn't* do that.

C: It's like pretending you're God and you're saying, "The world has to be destroyed."

T: Right. Except instead of saying, "The world has to be destroyed," you're saying, "People shouldn't cheat at soccer."

C: A lot of people do it though. It's kind of a free country, too.

T: What do you mean by that?

I knew what John meant but it's helpful to get the client to verbalize their rational ideas.

C: People are free and they can do whatever they want.

T: It would be nice if people would do the right thing, wouldn't it?

C: A lot do the right thing.

T: That's right. But they don't *have to,* do they?

C: Because they're the best and they think they can do anything. Like Mike, he got adopted when he was five and now he has a mom and dad. Then he used his hands on the last goal and everybody was happy but that was still cheating.

T: So they were happy even though he cheated to win. And you were kind of mad about that.

C: They say he can do anything.

T: Well, it is true that people can do what they want, pretty much. But it would be nice if people didn't cheat. Kind of like we said last time, "I wish they wouldn't use hands but if they really want to they can anyway." Like you said, "It's a free country and people can do what they want." Can you think of a time since the last time we talked where you've gotten angry about something other than soccer?

C: Like people swearing? People use the "S" word, the "F" word.

T: Right on the field, huh?

C: I know one kid who swears a lot.

T: So you end up feeling how about people swearing? Do you end up feeling angry?

C: Kind of.

T: Kind of angry.

C: I'm kind of used to it.

T: Let me ask you this. Listen real close because this is important. If you had to rate how angry you might feel if people swore, if you rated if between zero, which means not angry at all, and 100, how angry would you be?

C: About 50.

T: About 50. Let me ask you another question. How angry do you think it's Okay to feel if people swear? What number would you give that? Do you understand what I mean?

C: Yeah. I'd rate it a little bit higher.

T: So you don't even get as angry as you think it's Okay to get when people swear. Is that kind of what you are saying?

C: Yeah.

T: Okay.

The goal of this procedure is to determine if the client is unhealthily angry at other people or healthily irritated at their behavior. I asked John first to rate how angry he was [50]. He then reported that he felt it would be appropriate to be even a little angrier than 50. Because his rating was below what he considered a healthy level of anger, it is a pretty good indication that his response is healthy for the situation.

C: My mom would probably be at 100.

T: Your mom would be all the way to 100. She doesn't allow any swearing at all. That's probably a good idea. So what you're saying is that even though you get a little bit angry, it's a level of anger that you feel is about right for what happened. And it's Okay to get a little bit angry. We call that irritated. Do you know what irritated means?

C: It means that you're sort of angry but not really angry.

T: Yeah. You're a little upset that people are acting in a way you don't like but you're not really, really angry, like you're ready to hit something.

C: It's like I'm bothered by it.

T: That's a good word. Bothered.

C: Because I don't like to hear other people talk that way, swearing and all that, like they think everybody talks like that.

T: You think they want you to swear.

C: They want everybody to act the same way as they act.

T: What would it mean if they decided that because you don't do what they want you to do—like you don't swear—do you think they would really stop liking you?

C: No.

T: Probably not. If they were really friends, they wouldn't stop liking you. Let me ask you this: Now just pretend for a second, what if they stopped liking you? What would that prove about you?

C: I'd be kind of sad.

T: Okay. you'd be sad because you might not have as many friends to play with. But let me ask you this, would it mean that you're a rotten person?

C: No.

T: How come?

C: Because I don't want to say swears just because other kids do.

T: And that would just mean that you don't always go along with what everybody else does. That's Okay.

C: My mom won't let me swear.

T: Sometimes other people just aren't going to like us. Wouldn't it be kind of boring if everybody liked us. Let me ask you this, can we do anything to make people always like us?

C: Not really.

T: Probably not. And the really important part is that what other people think of us isn't as important as we sometimes make it out to be. Do you know what I mean? Can you explain what I mean by that?

C: Can you say that again?

T: Sure. What other people think of us isn't really as important as we make it out to be sometimes. Because we think, "If so and so doesn't like me it means I'm a real nerd or a dork." And it really doesn't mean that, does it? See if you can explain that to me.

C: Just because somebody calls you a name, you don't have to get mad about it.

T: You know what I say about that? If somebody called you a watermelon, it wouldn't make you a watermelon, would it? That's kind of silly isn't it? If somebody calls you a dork, big deal.

C: It's a free country.

T: That's right. You don't have to get mad at all.

Summary of Week Three

John appeared to be making good progress with his anger. The latter half of the session was spent assessing his self-acceptance. Many students feel that if others don't accept them, they can't accept themselves. John does not appear to suffer from this dire need for approval, which is a positive indicator for his overall emotional development.

A 9-Year-Old Girl Upset About Her Parents' Separating

Therapist: Albert Ellis, Ph.D.

This is the first and only session I had with a 9-year-old girl who was brought into therapy because, unlike her 11-year-old sister, she was quite angry and anxious about her parents fighting with each other, arranging to be separated, and at her mother's anger toward her. Her father, a 37-year-old teacher, had five sessions with me to alleviate his anger and anxiety about the difficult situation with his wife. He was learning REBT methods and successfully using them, and suggested that I have a session with his daughter "Mary," to help her cope with her problems about her parents. I agreed to have a session with Mary, and him, so that I might help her with her difficulties and also show him how to use REBT with Mary. I do this by having one or a few sessions with children when the parents are present, to teach them how to deal, educationally and practically, with their children. I assume that they are steadily around their children, can see their emotional upsets as they are occurring, and can forthrightly intervene with REBT to show the children how to be significantly less disturbed as well as, in the future, less disturbable (Ellis, 1999, 2000, 2001a, 2001b).

Mary is an attractive 9-year-old girl who is doing well in school, gets along nicely with her father, sister, and friends, and does not have a history of disturbing herself. Within the last several months, particularly after she learned that her parents were about to separate, she became anxious and somewhat depressed. During the session, she often spoke softly and I, who have a hearing difficulty, had some trouble hearing her. Her father, however, kept prompting her to speak up, and she usually did so when he prompted her.

THERAPIST: (To Mary's father) And how old is Mary, now?

FATHER: She's nine.

T: Nine. And in what grade?

F: She's in the fourth grade now.

T: Fourth grade. All right. (To Mary) What would you like to talk about?

MARY: Hmmm . . .

T: Anything bothering you?

M: Not much.

T: No? You're okay? (to Father) Well, what do you think it would be best for her to talk about?

F: Mary, would you like to talk about how you're feeling about what's going on in the family right now?

M: Uh. Uh.

F: Maybe about how you feel about the family breaking up? How you feel about me and mommy right now?

T: Yeah. How do you feel about your father and mother?

M: They fight a lot.

T: Oh. And how do you feel about their fighting?

M: Sad.

T: Yeah, you feel sad about that?

M: Uh-huh.

T: Are you upset about it?

M: I'm sad about it.

T: You're sad about it. That's okay but we don't want you to be upset, because . . . What do you tell yourself when they fight? What are you saying to yourself about their fighting?

M: Maybe they can work out their problems.

T: Yeah. Well, that's right. They may be able to, but suppose they're not. Suppose they don't work out their problems and they separate. How would you feel about that?

M: I don't know.

T: You'd have some feeling. Would you like that or not like it?

M: I wouldn't like it.

T: You wouldn't like it. Right? And you wouldn't like it because . . . Why wouldn't you like it? Let's suppose you live with one of them. Which one would you rather live with?

M: My mother.

T: Yes. All right, so you might live with your mother and then your father would see you regularly. You know, he'd visit you and you'd visit him? How would that be?

M: Okay.

T: That would be okay. And how about being separated from your sister? How would that be?

M: Sad.

T: Yeah well, that's okay if you're just sad. As long as you're not too upset about it. Because when things happen to us that we don't like we feel sad. But then you could also feel very angry and very depressed and very anxious. But if you only feel sad that would be okay. Do you think if you separated would . . . if they separated . . . and you were with your mother, you would go to the same school?

M: No.

T: She'd go to a different school?

F: That's right.

T: And how would that be to go to a different school?

M: It would feel different because I wouldn't be in the same school and I wouldn't know anyone there.

T: Yeah, I see, but you'd get to know people there. How far is that school?

F: It would be in Long Island.

T: So the mother would live in Long Island.

F: That's right.

T: And she's now in the Bronx. So it would be a different school system?

F: Altogether.

T: But the system is pretty good, isn't it?

F: It's a better system. That's one reason she's going there.

T: Yeah. You see it would be a good school system and you would make friends there. And Long Island is a nice place to live, you know. It's better than the Bronx. You live on Walton Avenue. I was raised in the Bronx. What's that near?

F: It's near Fordham Road.

T: Oh I see. So that's not a bad . . .

F: No, it's a pretty good neighborhood.

T: Yes, that's not a bad area of the Bronx, but Long Island's even better. Would they have an apartment?

F: They'd probably be living in an apartment, yes.

T: Yes. So you'd live with your mother. And how do you get along with your mother?

M: Very well.

T: Yeah. So that's okay. How do you get along with your father?

M: Very well, also.

T: Yes. So you get along with both of them.

M: Yes.

T: So it would be sad if they lived apart. But lots of parents live apart, you know. And how do you get along with your sister?

M: Very well, also.

T: Yeah. And would you miss her if you live with your mother?

M: Yes.

T: But you'll still see her, you know. You'll still visit with her as though you wouldn't really be separated from her. You'd see her every week or every other week or something like that, you see. And how about your friends? Do you have good friends at school?

M: Yes.

T: And would you miss them?

M: Yes.

T: But you could see some of them, too. You see, if you visit with your father, you could see some of your friends there. And then you'd make new friends. Do you like people? You like friends?

M: Yes.

T: And you'd be able to make friends?

M: Yes.

T: Yes. So you see you're doing pretty well. You sound pretty happy to me. Is there anything that really bothers you aside from your father and mother fighting? Anything else that bothers you?

M: No, not much.

T: No. So, you sound pretty good. I see lots of other children and they're bothered very much. They're very unhappy. They make themselves unhappy. But you sound like you're adjusting to the situation. And do you accept the fact that many fathers and mothers don't get along together. Do you accept that fact?

M: Yes.

T: Yes. Because that's true. You probably have some friends whose father and mothers are separated or don't get along. Don't you?

M: Yes.

T: Yeah. And they get by. You see it's *not* so terrible. How do you like school?

M: I like it a lot.

T: So you do well in school and you like studying and going to classes?

M: Yes.

T: Do you know what you want to be later on in life?

M: No.

T: No. You're young. You can decide later. What sort of subjects do you like most?

M: Art and science.

T: Science, yeah. Right. That's good. So maybe someday you'll be a scientist. We don't know. And what sort of subjects do you not like?

M: Math and social studies.

T: Social studies?

M: Yes.

T: Yes. But if you keep at them, you'll get them into your head and you'll do well. It's a matter of persistence, you see. You really keep at the math and social studies. You'll get to know them better and better and you'll even come to enjoy them. What sort of activities do you like?

M: Sports.

T: Sports. Watching them on TV?

M: No, I like to play basketball.

T: Basketball? And you have a basketball team at school?

M: No.

T: No, but you like to play basketball?

M: Yes.

T: Yes, I see. So, that's pretty enjoyable. Do you like television or movies?

M: Yes.

T: Yes. Right. Do you like reading?

M: Not much.

T: No, you don't like reading that much. But if you keep at it, it becomes easier and easier and you will like it, you see. Most people have a little difficulty with it but then they persist and they get to like it very much, you see, especially if they read stories and all kinds of other things. And, of course, it helps you in school if you keep reading. You learn new information, you see. Is there anything else in life that you dislike or you don't like?

M: Not much.

T: But what would you like to see changed in your life? Is there anything you'd like to see changed?

M: Not much.

T: Not too much?

M: Uh uh.

T: So you like your friends and you like the school and you like your sister and you like both your mother and your father. Right?

M: Yes.

T: That's a pretty good life. You're doing better than most people, you see. But let's get back to the fighting between your parents. When they're fighting with each other, are they very loud? Do they call each other names? What do they do?

M: They scream at each other a lot.

T: They call each other names?

M: They stomp around and stuff.

T: Yeah. And how do you feel when that happens?

M: Mad and scared a little.

T: Yeah. And what do you get mad at? That they *shouldn't* be that way? They *should* calm down and shouldn't fight?

M: Because I get sick of hearing them fight a lot. But I know they're going to fight anyway.

T: That's right. You can't stop them. You can stop yourself from fighting with other children or even with your parents, but you can't stop your parents from fighting. They might stop it someday and if they were separated from each other they might fight less. You see, that's one of the reasons that they're separating. Then they wouldn't be around each other and they'd both have their own life and fight less. But you can't stop people from fighting, so you say to yourself, "I wish they wouldn't fight but if they do, they do. I'm not gonna upset myself about it. It doesn't mean anything about me." Because they're not fighting over you, are they?

M: No.

T: No. They're fighting because they have differences with each other. That's what people do. When they marry they think they'll get along very well and for awhile they usually do. But then something happens between them and one thinks one way and the one thinks the other way and they have differences, you see. And they don't agree and then they argue with each other. Do they hit each other?

M: No.

T: Do they ever hit you?

M: Not during a fight.

T: Not during a fight. But when do you get hit?

M: Like when I don't do something that I'm supposed to do. Like my room or something like that.

T: Oh, I see. And who's the one that usually hits you?

M: Mommy.

T: Yeah. So she gets angry when you don't clean your room or something like that.

M: Yeah.

T: And how do you feel when she hits you?

M: Angry at her.

At the opening of this session, Mary acts as if everything is okay and that she has no great problems—as children often do. I listen carefully and reassure her that she seems to be doing quite well under difficult conditions. I indicate that even the coming separation of her parents is not as bad as it could be, and by my tone and manner I show her that I think she is quite capable of handling it. Probably because I persist and am unthreatening, Mary begins to open up about her real problems, especially her parents' fighting and her mother's anger at her for not cleaning her room.

Although Mary's anger does not seem to be too serious, REBT considers anger, as opposed to healthy feelings of annoyance and irritation, a real emotional problem. So I actively-directly start to educate Mary about what anger truly is and how she and others can deal with it without making themselves angry.

T: Yeah. All right, because you see what you're saying to yourself is (1) "I don't like her hitting me" and that's okay. We don't want you to like it. It's uncomfortable. It's frustrating to get hit. So you're saying (1) "I don't like it" and then (2) "She *shouldn't* do that." So then you get angry at her. Now it's better if she doesn't hit you, but sometimes people do what they had better not do, you see. They get angry, they get upset. Your mother gets upset when you don't clean your room or something like that and then she says to herself, "My daughter isn't doing the right thing, cleaning her room, and she *should*." Then she makes herself angry, you see. People get angry, they make themselves angry when they *demand*. Instead of saying, "I wish this would happen," they say, "It's *got to* happen. It *must* happen." And when they dislike something, they often tell themselves, "It *must not* be this way." And then they get very angry, you see. And that's what your mother is doing at times. She's upsetting herself instead of just telling herself, "I wish Mary would act better." She's saying, "Mary *should*, she *ought*, she has *got* to act better." Now do you see the difference between these two statements?

M: Yes.

[*JW: I try to get into the habit of asking children to repeat the concepts I teach back to me as a means of checking on their comprehension. Some clients are great at saying, "Yes, I understand" when, in fact, they don't really comprehend what you're trying to teach them.*]

T: Yeah. And whenever you tell yourself that people *should, must* act better and they *don't,* then you feel angry. And then you yell and you scream and you sometimes hit them. So your mother is taking you too seriously when you don't clean your room or something like that. She's upsetting herself and she could learn not to upset herself, but right now she's doing it. She's used to acting that way, you see. And she may be right about the room. Maybe you are careless. Do you clean your room okay or not clean it okay?

M: I do clean it okay.

T: You do? But she wants it even better?

M: Yes.

T: Well, she may be what we call a perfectionist. She may demand in her head that, "You must do it better. You must do it better." Then she'll upset herself, you see. She has too high standards of cleaning. Does she use the same standards on herself? Does she clean the room perfectly well when she cleans it.

M: No. She doesn't clean. Her desk has all dirt around it. Piles and everything.

T: So, she doesn't clean it? She makes you clean it?

M: No, she makes me clean my room and she says my room is worse than hers and she hasn't cleaned it for two years.

T: But you do clean it regularly?

M: Yes.

T: Yeah. But it's not good enough.

M: No.

T: According to her. But that's her problem: that she's *demanding* that you must clean it better than you're doing. Maybe she's guilty about not cleaning it herself. Why does she never clean it?

M: I don't know.

T: She doesn't have the time?

M: I don't know, because she's always doing like records for her class and stuff.

T: Records for . . . ?

F: She's always doing her own work. Records for her class and things.

T: So she's very busy with her own work?

M: Yes.

T: Yeah. But your mother works and also takes care of you and your sister somewhat. Is that right?

M: Yes.

T: So she has a very busy life, you see. And your father works, too. Is he okay about the rooms?

M: Yes.

T: Yeah. He doesn't bother you.

M: No. But he helps us sometimes but she goes and screams at him for helping us.

F: I help them clean the rooms and my wife will scream at me for helping clean their rooms.

T: (to Mary's father) So sometimes you help but her mother doesn't help because she's too busy?

F: Right.

T: Is that right? So therefore she doesn't help. But your mother does have a busy life doesn't she?

M: Yes.

T: Yeah. And she does have a lot of work to do with her own work, right?

M: Yes.

T: So she wants you to clean the room, while your father is more lenient and he helps you sometimes.

M: Yes.

T: Right. And do you think your mother is right or wrong about that?

M: Wrong.

T: Yeah. But people are often wrong. That's their nature, to often be wrong. They make mistakes. Your mother is a fallible human. She makes errors. And she does have a busy life, you see. So she may neglect helping you somewhat but she thinks you're big enough and bright enough to help yourself. See, she has faith in you but when you don't do the cleaning the right way then she makes herself upset about it, which she doesn't have to do. But she does upset herself. And then she yells or screams or hits you or something like that. Now when she does that you'd better say to yourself, "My mother has a problem. Too bad. I wish she didn't have that problem, to be perfectionistic, to keep after me, etc. I wish she were more like my father in that respect. But that's too bad and I can live with it." Now could you tell yourself something like that?

M: Yes.

T: Don't say, "I can't *stand* it! It's *awful!*" Because then you'll feel worse. If you say, "I can't *stand* it! I can't *stand* it!" then you'll feel it's very, very unfair and you *won't* be able to stand it and you'll make yourself upset. While if you say, "Too bad. That's the way my mother is. I wish she weren't, but she is," then you'll be less upset. You see. And you'll accept her with her wrongness when you think she's wrong. You see the difference between, "Too bad" and "That's awful! I can't stand it!" They're different. Do you see the difference?

M: Uh-huh.

[JW: Once again, it might be a good idea to ask the client to clarify his or her under-standing at this point. Ask the client, "Explain what we're talking about using your own words."]

T: So if we can get you to say to yourself when things go wrong at school, or with your friends, or with sports, or with your mother, or even your father, "Too bad. I don't like it but I can live with it and still be happy even with this wrongness that they're doing." Then you'll be a happier person. But you have to have that kind of philosophy. "Too bad. Too bad. But I can *accept* it and live with it. I don't have to make myself miserable even when people act badly, which they do. Because your mother is not the only one who acts badly, is she?

M: No.

T: No. Other people do. Your sister does at times. Your father does at times. People are fallible. They make errors. They do the wrong things. Very, very often. If you read the newspaper or listen to television, you'll see how the world is. The president makes mistakes and everybody makes mistakes. And I'm sure your teachers at times make mistakes. Don't they?

M: Yes.

T: Yeah. Now do you upset yourself about that?

M: No.

T: No, you don't have to. You say, "Too bad. I wish they wouldn't make mistakes, but they do. Tough. But I don't have to make myself miserable and demand that they not make mistakes. Because if I demand it and they still make mistakes then I will upset myself. "They *must* not treat me that way! They *must* not make mistakes!" You see, that's your *demand*. Instead of, "I wish they wouldn't treat me that way but if they do, they do. Too bad. Too bad. I can live with it. I don't have to make myself very upset." See, that's a good philosophy, which will keep you happier. While if you say, "I can't stand it! It's *awful*! It's *terrible*!" then you'll make yourself more unhappy. And when you say that, and make yourself miserable, your mother and other people act even worse, you see. So you have to change what you can change. Whenever anyone acts badly, you try to talk to them and get them to change it. That's okay. But if they don't, they don't. You can't always persuade them. If you talk to your mother, you don't always convince her, do you?

M: No.

I judge, clinically, that Mary is an intelligent child who is only moderately disturbed, and I take the chance that I can clearly and quickly show her how most people foolishly enrage themselves about others' mistakes. I show her how her mother seems to do this and sometimes does it unfairly, and how Mary can prevent herself from reacting angrily to her mother's perfectionism, by accepting her mother's mistaken behavior and not *demanding* that she act fairly.

T: Or you often can't convince your father or anybody else. People will do what they do. And your mother thinks she's right, incidentally. She thinks it's correct when she gets after you and even hits you. She thinks she's right, even though she may not be right. You see, people think that way. When they do something bad they often think, "I'm okay. That was correct what I did." They fool themselves, you see. That's the human race. They very frequently act that way. They don't want to admit their mistakes so they blame you. It happens all the time and it's unfair. And that's what you are telling yourself. You are saying, "It's unfair when my mother treats me that way." Aren't you? To yourself? "It's unfair."

M: Yes.

T: And you may be right. It may be unfair. But then you're also saying, "She *must not* act unfairly." But you can't stop people at times from acting unfairly. They do. You see. They're fallible. They make errors. They act unfairly. Everybody does at times. Even you at times will be a little unfair to your sister or to somebody else. That's human nature. And your problem is to accept that. Not to like it but to accept that and not to tell yourself, "It *must* not be that way. They must be fair! They must be fair! They must be fair! " That won't work. It would be nice if people were fair. It would be very nice, but they often aren't. Is that true?

M: Yes.

T: So you have to live in a world where your mother and other people, at times but not always, are going to be unfair. What can you do?

M: Nothing.

T: You can't change them, you see. But if you don't make yourself angry at them and you just calmly talk to them and don't angrily blame them back, then sometimes they change. But if you say to your mother, "You're unfair and you *shouldn't be* unfair," she'll get upset about that and then she may act worse, you see. Whenever you criticize people they often act worse. And I think your mother often doesn't see that she is unfair. She thinks you're unfair when you don't clean the room, so she thinks *you're* wrong and you think *she's* wrong and then we get nowhere. So your problem is to tell yourself, "Maybe my mother is wrong about this. So she's wrong. Too bad. I can live with it. And when I have children, I'll act differently." Do you want to marry ultimately and have children of your own?

M: Yes. Yes.

T: You do. Right. And if you follow what we're talking about, this philosophy I'm advocating, then when your children act badly you won't upset yourself about it. You'll say "Too bad. Children often act badly. Tough. I don't like it but I can accept it," you see. While if you get angry, like your mother does, you'll say, "They *shouldn't* be that way. They *shouldn't* be that way!" And then you'll scream and yell at your kids and you may even hit them, and that won't do them any good. So many bad things exist in life; many good things also exist, because most of your life sounds pretty good to me. Your school is okay. Sports are okay. You get along with your sister. And mostly you get along with your father.

M: Yes.

Because REBT follows the educational and preventative model, rather than the medical model, I keep showing Mary how she and other people commonly upset themselves. So if she wants to live happily, now and in the future, she'd better see that this is so and change her self-angering philosophy and actions.

T: Does your father do anything you don't like?

M: Not really. But he smokes a lot.

T: Yeah, I see. So he's wrong about that. He's foolish for smoking because he could get lung cancer. But you have to try to convince him that, "That's stupid Daddy, but you're not a stupid, rotten person. You'd be much better off and I would be better off if you stopped smoking." See. Because he *acts* foolishly at times. He's a bright man but he does some foolish things like smoking. And someday, if you don't get angry at him and you just keep pointing out what happens to people who smoke, you may help him. They get lung cancer and things like that. We hope he'll stop smoking, you see. But this just proves that your father is a bright and competent man but he does some foolish acts. Like smoking. Most people do. They smoke. They drink. They eat too much. People often do that. They're not that disciplined. He gets pleasure out of the smoking so he forgets about the pain he may get later. And he'd better remind himself, and every once in a while you'd better remind him, about the pain of smoking. Because he's just concentrating on its pleasure. That's what people do. They go for something that satisfies them right now and they forget what will happen in the future. So his smoking is pleasurable. He enjoys it but he's ignoring the fact that it will do him in later, which it well may. What don't you like about the smoking?

M: That he's always outside. And he goes outside a lot and when he goes out mommy starts to get mad and stuff like that.

T: You go outside the apartment?

F: Yes, I smoke outside the apartment.

T: So you're not there when you're smoking?

F: No.

T: And how often do you do that?

F: It depends. Two or three times a . . . Well, it depends. Mainly I'll go out before I go to bed and I'll have a cigarette. I'll take down the garbage and I'll have a cigarette. Once or twice in the evening.

T: And you stay out for how long?

F: About seven minutes; ten minutes. As long as it takes to smoke a cigarette.

T: And then you come back?

F: Right.

T: Right. So he does come back all the time.

F: Yeah.

T: He's not leaving the house. He just goes out for a smoke and he would be better off if he didn't. And someday, we hope, he'll give up that habit. That's a bad habit. Drinking too much, eating too much, smoking too much, gambling too much—they're all bad habits. They get us into trouble. What else don't you like about your father?

M: Not much.

T: Oh. I see. The main thing is the smoking.

M: Yes.

T: Yeah. But at least he doesn't smoke when you're around so he doesn't blow the smoke in your face. Right?

M: Sometimes when we are walking to some places he still smokes.

T: Oh, I see. But that's out in the open air. So that won't affect you. If he does it indoors, then you may get harmed by the smoking. But as long as he does it outside, the air takes away the smoke, you see. So it still may harm him when he does it outside but it really won't harm you. It just harms him. But if he does it indoors, then you'd better get after him and complain about it without getting yourself upset about it, you see. That would be preferable. It would be better if he stopped. We're not denying that. It would be preferable if your mother didn't get angry and hit you. But you can't make people act well all the time. They won't do that practically ever. They all have their errors, their mistakes, their failings. All humans. What don't you like about what you do? Anything about your behavior you don't like?

M: No.

T: No. So you're okay. You don't smoke?

M: No.

T: And you don't drink?

M: No.

T: And you do your homework?

M: Yes.

T: Yeah. So she has pretty good habits?

F: Yep.

T: Yeah. So that's very good. You see, you're doing better than most children your age. Some of them even smoke. Usually, they are a little older than you. But they don't do their homework and they fight and get into trouble. So it sounds to me that you're doing pretty well under difficult conditions. And if you follow what we're talking about and stop upsetting yourself, then you'll do even better. You'll be a happier person, even though the world will still have many rotten things in it. Because it will. It frequently does. Is there anything you want to ask me about anything? Because I could give you some answers.

M: No. Not much.

T: Right. Anything you want to ask your father or work out with your father while he's here?

M: No.

T: No. So the main thing you'd like to change is your mother and father fighting and your mother getting after you at times to clean your room and sometimes hitting you. Those are the two main things. Right?

M: Uh-huh. Yes.

T: All right. But as you and I said, if they don't get along with each other, if they fight, I don't know how you're going to stop them. You can't control them. They may be wrong but you're not going to change them. So you have to put up with that and if they live apart, then you won't see much fighting. That will be an advantage. You see, if they're together they'll fight, but they may get along much better if they live apart. Many parents do. If they live apart they can be friendlier and get along a lot better. And if your mother lives with you, she may be less perfectionistic and may not get after you that much about your room and things like that. She may be calmer, once she separates from your father. She may be calmer and less upset, and she may treat you better. See, that's very possible. You see what I mean? Once she calms down and is away from your father, she may treat you a lot better. And she'll be able to pay more attention to you because your sister won't be around that much. She'll only have one of you. And her life will be easier and less complicated. And she'll go to work and then she'll come home and take care of you. Is that what will likely happen?

M: Yes.

T: Yeah.

F: I suppose, yes.

T: Yeah.

F: That's what will happen.

T: And you'll have somebody else to take care of you, too. A babysitter or somebody?

M: I don't know because sometimes I come home by myself.

T: Yes, but you're able to take care of yourself alone, aren't you?

M: Yes.

T: You can get along when you're in the house alone?

M: Yes.

T: Can you cook?

M: Yes.

T: See, that's pretty good at your age. And you can do your homework?

M: Yes.

T: Right. And you can look at TV.

M: Yes.

T: So if you're home alone and your mother is still working, you can still enjoy yourself and get by. You see, it won't be so bad and, as I said before, if you're living with your mother you'll make new friends: (1) at school and (2) frequently in the neighborhood you'll have friends. And living in Long Island—a good place to live. One of the best. In the whole country, Long Island is one of the best places. Are you afraid to be in a new place?

M: No.

T: You're pretty sure you could get along in a new school?

M: Yes.

T: Yeah. You're sociable and you make friends and the kids in Long Island will be okay. Your present school is okay?

M: Yes.

T: Yeah. So that's all right. But the school in Long Island will be a good school, too. Maybe even better than your present one, you know. What else do you think may bother you? Have we omitted anything that really bothers you? Because we want you to be able to cope with life. What else do you think may come up that would be bothersome?

M: I don't know.

T: You're not worried about anything?

M: Not much.

T: No. So that's a pretty good attitude, you see. If you have the attitude, "I can handle it. I can take care of it," then whatever happens to you, you'll be okay. The children who say, "I can't handle it. I can't take care of it." But if you say, "I can handle a new school, I can handle a new neighborhood. I can get along with my mother maybe better. I can see my father and my sister. Whatever happens I can handle it. Whatever happens I can handle it!" That's what you can keep telling yourself until you really believe it. (to Mary's father) Is there anything you'd like to bring up about her and her problems?

F: I'm just concerned with Mary having to deal with other people's angry behavior, particularly when she does move. If that does come up.

T: If people are angry at her?

F: Yeah. If they behave in a particular way, abusively toward her. That's my concern. That she knows how she can handle it and that she'll be willing to speak up about it.

T: Yeah.

F: If it does come up.

T: (to Mary) Yes, that's right. Do you see what he's talking about? Because some people will get angry at you. Some will because you did something wrong and some because you did something right. They'll still get angry because they are demanding people. So you'd better understand that whenever anybody gets angry at you, your mother, your father, your sister, anybody, they're saying, first, that they think you're wrong. Now, they may be wrong about that, they're seeing you as doing the wrong thing. Not cleaning the room well enough or something like that. They think that you are wrong, and then they tell themselves, "You *shouldn't* be wrong. You *must* not do what I don't want you to do." That's what anger is. They want you to do this, and instead you do that. So they say to themselves, "Mary must not do that. She's no good." And they yell and scream and sometimes hit you. Because they're wrongly saying that you *must* do what they want you to do, you see. So what you can do is, first, realize that they are saying that to themselves. That they are demanding, demanding, demanding that you act differently. They are not just wishing and wanting, they're demanding. "Mary *must* act differently. She *must not* do that." So you say to yourself, "Maybe I did something wrong, maybe." Because maybe you didn't clean the room good enough or you didn't do something else. But you tell yourself, "I'm still okay. That's a wrong thing to do. But I can accept myself with my wrongness and then later maybe I'll change it." But *don't* tell yourself, "I'm no good because they're *telling me* I'm no good." You see, they'll say, (1) "Mary's wrong" and (2) "She's no good for being wrong." Now you can accept the first part, "Maybe I'm wrong. Maybe I'm wrong. Maybe I did the wrong thing, but *I'm* still okay. No matter what I do, I'm a good person because I am me, I exist and I have the right to do wrong things. I'm fallible. Once in a while I really do wrong things." So never put yourself down. You just tell yourself, "At the very worst, I did the wrong thing. Too bad! I'll try to change it later. Or stop doing it again." But you never say, "I'm no good. I'm no good." That's really wrong if you say that. Because then you'll tend to do worse. So you say to yourself, "They're angry at me. They're demanding that I do something other than I did. That's too bad. That's *their* problem. Not that they think that I'm wrong. They may be right about that. But they're upsetting themselves about it. They have a problem. Angry people have a problem. Angry people have a problem." You just say that to yourself, "Too bad. I'll try to show them that I'm okay." And that may work, but it also may not work. They may never agree. They may keep telling you, "You're no good! You're no good!" But you can say to yourself, "They're wrong about that. Even if I did badly, I'm okay. I'm still okay. I can accept myself with my bad behavior. Then later I'll change it. But I'm never a louse, I'm never a worm, I'm never a no-goodnik. I am just a human who this time may have done something stupid or wrong or that they don't like." So you accept *yourself* all the time. Not what you *do*. If it's wrong, it's wrong. But you never put *yourself* down because they're putting you down. You never agree with them, "I'm no good. I'm no good. Yes, they're right. I'm no good." You never do that. And you tell yourself, "Too bad that they're very angry because they have a problem. They're too demanding. They're too perfectionistic. I wish they didn't make themselves angry, but they do. And as I said before, I can live with their problem and not upset myself about it. And then as I do that, I'll try to assert myself and get them to change, but I may or may not succeed." Especially if the people who are angry at you have authority—if they're a teacher or a principal or a boss or your mother. You may not be able to change them because they may not listen. You see, they may have problems. Now do you understand what I just said?

M: Yes.

T: So, you can always accept *you,* even when you do something wrong. And you can accept the fact that angry people have a problem. "They have a problem by being demanding, and making themselves angry at me. Too bad. I wish they didn't but they do. So even when I do something wrong and they're screaming and yelling at me, that's their problem. They're demanding, demanding, demanding. Tough. Too bad. But I never have to put myself down, and I can accept the fact that they have problems. People have problems. My mother, my father, my sister, other people and some of my friends who get angry at me at times, have their own problems, but that's too bad." It's not *terrible,* it's not *awful,* it's not *horrible.* But it's a pain in the butt! So I'm not denying that it's bad. It's not good when people yell and scream and hit you. It's bad, but that's what people with problems do. They act badly. Then later they often calm down. Your mother yells for a while and then she stops it. She hits you and then she stops it. But for the time being, she and other people may be wrongly angry at you. They may put you down. "You're no good! You're no good!" Don't agree with that, but tell yourself, instead, "Even if I do badly, I'm okay. I'm a good person who acted badly. Now let me do better next time." Now is there anything about that that you don't understand?

M: No.

T: No. But you have to say it to yourself over and over, until you really think it in your head. You see, your father will help you with that. He knows how to do this. So tell him when you get upset. When you get upset about anything, you can talk to your father and tell him what you're upset about. Tell him what you're angry about or if you're putting yourself down about anything, he'll help you change that, and help you get a good philosophy. He's learning how to do that himself and he'll be able to show you how to do it. So don't hesitate to talk to him about it. And sometimes, if you're not too upset, you can talk to your mother, your teachers, or to other kids about their poor behavior, and sometimes they'll change, but don't count on it. Sometimes they won't change. Anything we may have omitted so far?

M: No.

T: All right. Anything you think you're still going to have trouble with?

M: No.

T: All right. Well, again I think that you're doing very well under difficult conditions. Because you do have a mother and father who fight and not every mother and father fight. And you do have a mother who gets angry at you and at times hits you and you may have to be separated from your sister. We don't know yet, but that may occur. So you have practical problems to solve but they're not *awful,* they're not *terrible,* and again we go back to what you tell yourself, "I can handle it. I can handle it. I can handle it. Whatever comes up, I am a bright little girl and I can think about it and handle it." See, if you have that attitude, that philosophy, you'll handle it pretty well. You're actually doing pretty well at handling it already. Anything else you want to bring up?

F: No. No, I think we've pretty much covered everything that we had to speak about.

T: Right. And as I said before, if you get in any trouble, if you feel upset, talk to your father. And if you want to talk to me again about it, just write down the things that are bothering you, because you may forget them. Make little notes to yourself. And then if your father brings you back here, if you want to come, then we'll go over those things that bother you. Anything that bothers you we can talk about. But, first, you can talk to your father about it and most of the time he'll be able to help you. Sometimes you can talk to your mother about it, but we're not sure how she'll react.

F: Okay.

T: Okay?

M: Yes.

T: Okay. It was very good talking to you. You think about it. You have a good head. If you think about these things you can stop upsetting yourself. Even when life has bad things in it.

F: Okay.

T: Okay.

M: Goodbye.

T: Goodbye.

I thought that this was a fairly successful session with Mary and her father, although she by no means spoke up as much as I would have liked her to do and she may have been restricted in displaying some of her feelings because of her father's presence. Mary did not choose to see me again but had two brief phone sessions with me—once, a few weeks later, when she got angry at her mother. I repeated the same kind of REBT statements I had made about her and her mother creating their own anger and she quickly calmed down. Two months after that, she had another brief phone session with me, when she actually moved with her mother to Long Island and she was depressed because of the separation from her father and angry that she, rather than her sister, was forced to live with her mother. Again, she was able to accept this "terrible" situation and live with it.

According to her father, who saw Mary regularly and continued the same kind of REBT education with her that I had started, Mary adjusted to her parents' separation and to moving to Long Island very well. She also handled her mother's angry outbursts for the most part and made herself much less resentful of her mother's "unfairness." Her father was enthusiastic about her changes and thought that they proved that REBT could work nicely for both him and Mary. He stopped quarreling with his wife, although she continued to bait him when they were in contact, and he took their separation and subsequent divorce quite well. With the father's help, Mary gradually increasingly accepted the REBT principles I tried to teach her in the one session and two brief phone sessions that we had.

The main REBT philosophies that I tried to teach Mary were, first, unconditional self-acceptance (USA). I tried to show her that she could always accept herself even when her behaviors—such as her anger at her mother—were far from ideal. She, like all people, was a fallible human, who sometimes performed badly but was never a bad person.

Second, I tried to teach Mary that she could achieve unconditional other-acceptance (UOA). She could accept the fact that people—especially her mother—had their own problems and were forgivable, even when not likeable. She couldn't change people and she had darn well better accept that.

Third, I tried to enable Mary to have high frustration tolerance. She could realize that conditions were not as bad as she at first thought them to be. She could *handle*, without *liking*, unfortunate changes in her life. She could convince herself "too bad" instead of awfulizing about poor conditions.

Because Mary was only 9 years old and not too likely to learn how to dispute her Irrational Beliefs, I gave her—as I often do with youngsters—rational coping statements to think about and repeat to herself. I, and later her father, helped her to keep repeating to herself when undesirable things happened, "It's not the end of the world!" "I can handle it," "I wish things were better, but I can't *command* them to be," "I make *myself* angry and my mother doesn't make me angry at her." By my and her father's repetitions of rational coping statements like these, and especially by strongly repeating them to herself, Mary was able to improve her feelings and behaviors in the face of some real continued difficulties.

References

Ellis, A. (1999). *How to be happy and remarkably less disturbable*. Atascadero, CA. Impact.

Ellis, A. (2000). *How to control your anxiety before it controls you*. New York: Citadel.

Ellis, A. (2001a). *Feeling better, getting better, staying better*. Atascadero, CA: Impact.

Ellis, A. (2001b). *Overcoming destructive beliefs, feelings, and behaviors*. Amherst, NY: Prometheus Books.

A 17-Year-Old Adolescent Male With Family Problems

Therapist: Thomas F. Mooney, Ed.D.

The following is a transcription of the third session with a 17-year-old young man, "Jack," who entered therapy as a result of a family crisis. The crisis was precipitated by his realizing that his relationships with his family were being seriously jeopardized by the amount of time, energy, and money that he was spending trying to nurture his "friends." Initially he was very upset, suffering much guilt and anguish as he realized how his behavior had alienated various family members.

This session deals mostly with the therapist going over the musturbatory Belief of this client that he "must be accepted and approved" by people whom he considered important. Pollack (1998) addresses this issue with his concept of "cool pose." Harris (1998) in her book, *The Nurture Assumption,* raises new issues as to the power of the peer group in influencing behavior.

The advantage of an REBT approach to issues of peer group influence is conceptualized by the ABC model, with Point A representing the client's peer group, Point B being his Beliefs that he absolutely must have their approval, and Point C constituting his feelings and behaviors of self-downing when lacking the approval of his peers. This particular session focused mostly on those sentences that this young man was telling himself as to how crucial it was that his friends like him and approve of him, resulting in his giving too generously of his time, his car, and his money. After his initial "musts" of approval were isolated, disputing this belief was inaugurated and reframed. As the transcript will show, the client sees his "musts of acceptance" and realizes what great power these "musts" have on his dysfunctional behavior.

The client's use of the phrase "f—— 'em" is a form of disputation in this context, not an angry retaliation. This phrase enables him to take back his power over himself and bring his friendships to a choice level that is under his control.

The plan for follow-up sessions is to make sure that the client is freed of his musturbatory needs for acceptance so that he can make better choices with his time, money, and car and balance his free time with family and friends.

THERAPIST: Jack, this is third time that we have met. The first couple of times you were talking about spending a lot of time with your friends. You felt pretty bad about that because it excluded you from spending time with your family. You and I have talked about why it was so important to be with your friends. We were trying to tap into what those Belief systems were. So if we can kind of review that . . . When it was important to be with your friends, what were the main thoughts, what were the main Belief systems along the line of "It's important for me to be with my friends. I should be with my friends. I have to be with my friends. It's important they like me. I must have them liking me." Can you pick it up there, Jack?

CLIENT: I guess I could say that I felt like they just always wanted to use me for stuff. Like whenever they always ask me to give them rides all around town, and do all this special stuff like always borrowing money from me, always using me for somewhere . . .

T: But what allowed you to do that? You did it for them. What motivated you?

C: What motivated me was the fear of the fact that if I didn't do it for them, I thought I'd be really left out, and that they wouldn't like, like me as much anymore. Like if I didn't do that special thing for them, you know, always like fulfilling all their needs, what they wanted me to do for them, I thought they would get p—— off or upset.

T: It was important for you that they like you, accept you, because . . . ?

C: I don't know, it's just the way, how I feel about them. I care about them like, a little bit more than I care about myself, it seems like.

T: But can you see the sentences going off in your head, "I must have them like me"? Can you look back and see what that sentence was, "I must have them like me," or some form of that?

C: Hmm . . . yeah . . .

T: "I must be liked by them. I must have them like me. I must be accepted by them."

C: Pretty much that's it. Like I just always thought I had to do it, to have them like me.

T: To look back at it now, sentences that go through your head affect the way that you feel. You felt very positive. You felt like you really had to do these kinds of things. Your feelings, to a great extent, stem from what you think and the sentences that you tell yourself. So if we're looking at this once more here, your feelings were to bend over backwards to help them so that they would like you. But that Belief system inside of your head was some form of "I must win their approval," "They must like me" . . . Can you look back on that and see that sentence?

C: You mean when did I see it, when it came through my head like time-wise? I would say . . . ever since I got my car, and up until a little while ago, it wasn't a problem. Then it hit me that I felt I was being used, like they liked me and wanted to be with me because I had the car. It just wasn't for me. After the first or second time I came over and talked to you. And you, like, filled me in on that self-confidence stuff. And then I was starting to think that if they really did like me, they wouldn't care about all that other stuff. And so far it's worked.

T: Tell me what's different about your philosophy now, your thoughts now, about friends.

C: About friends . . . well, you gain some and you lose some I guess. The ones who stay with you through all of it are the only ones that matter. All the other ones who get p—— off at you for the simple fact that you're not going to let them borrow money, or take them to the party store, or drive them around. If they don't like you for you then f—— 'em. They don't matter.

T: When you were so busy spending so much time, effort, and money doing things to help them, did you like *you* very much?

C: No, I wouldn't say that. I don't know, it seemed like, I more like felt more like . . . well, if I do this, they'll be happy, but then I'll be broke. Or if I do this for them, they'll be happy but I've got to drive all the way over there, and I got to do this, and I got to do that. And it's an awful long drive. Like going to a concert, they always ask me to drive them and I'll say like, "I don't know, man," and they're like "Oh come on, man, let's go."

T: And you couldn't say "No" back then. You couldn't say "No" to them because . . .

C: They'd keep pushing it on. And the more they pushed it on, the more I would think that they're going to be p—— at me if I say "No" . . .

T: "I can't stand the idea of them being upset at me, I must have them like me, therefore I'll give, I'll give . . ."

C: Yeah . . .

T: "I can't stand the idea of them being upset at me"?

C: Yeah . . . pretty much.

T: Now on the basis of our talks so far, how are you viewing these kinds of things now?

C: It's like I said before, the only thing is, like my buddy Sara, she has a little of the same problems as I do. Like ever since she got her car, she's like noticed that because we hang out with the same people, and work with the same people and stuff; and . . . like . . . they would just . . . I don't exactly know how to explain it. There's other people there who have cars, you know, but they never drive them, they never went to town in theirs. It is always my car. Sara has felt like this, too.

T: But what I hear you saying differently now is that, "I've really seen where me giving so much of me to them, and they just took, then I didn't like me all that well."

C: Yeah.

T: "I overextended me, it cost money, because I falsely thought I needed their acceptance." What I hear you saying now is, "I can say 'No' to them, I can trust me, what's right for me. I can listen better to my inner sentences of what's right for me." Can you tell me what you're seeing more along that line now?

C: For me . . .

T: You can say "No" to them and not feel too bad? You're not worried or scared?

C: I've got more respect for myself now, in a way.

T: Let's stay a minute on that one . . . "I feel I respect me more"? Tell me more.

C: I get to do more of what I want instead of doing what they did. So they ask me what I'm doing that day, and they'll tell me what they're doing and like, "You want to drive? You want to go?" And I'm like "No." Before I would just kind of beat around the bush and not say "No."

T: Scared?

C: Yeah. Before I'd say, "Well, I don't know man, I'll see what's going down later." Then later on I'll have like four or five people come over because I told them the same thing. But now it's like I make the first plan that comes to mind, whether it's go over to my grandparents' house, go over to my dad's house, or whatever. Just in this past week, I went over and visited both of them, which I haven't done that forever, because my friends were always right there with me. I saw my dad last night. Well, not my dad, but my stepmom, my dad wasn't there, and I saw my grandparents last Sunday.

T: So you feel able to make better choices now.

C: Yeah. Better choices for myself, not choices made by my friends. Well, I never really made choices for my friends, I just did for my friends. I let them make the choices, but now I make choices freely, I guess you'd call it. I do my own thing, I don't like lock down with one person. Me and him always did everything and then like pretty much, I got sick of it after awhile because he's always counting on me to take him around. He's like, "Well, what's going down?" and I was just planning on going home, maybe sleeping or maybe going out with my girl-friend, and I'd tell him that. And he's like, "Oh come on, man, let's go out and do this." And then I'd go with him and actually we'd just end up driving around all the time, and it ain't fun, you know. I wasn't doing what I wanted and he was just always there with me. Like hey, he loves it because he's never at home and he's always doing something, and like I always felt I had to make sure that he's having fun for some reason. But now it's like, if we don't have fun, or if we do have fun, it's at my expense, you know, and I don't like to see that s—— go down. I try to make sure that it don't go down now.

T: But you're different now. It sounds like you are taking charge over you. You're listening more to what "I want." You've come to terms with it, you've changed "it's important they like me, I must do things so that I can win their acceptance." You're listening more to what's right for you, and feeling confident now?

C: Hmm, yeah.

T: More so?

C: More so than what, was before. Sometimes I still think about it. But I always try to stay true to my word and what I say to myself . . . That's the best way to go about it, I guess. Be true to yourself and if anyone has a problem with it, oh well.

T: So, what you kind of found out being accepted by your friends is not a real life or death?

C: No . . .

T: Are you finding that you've lost any friends?

C: Nope, I haven't lost any of my friends yet. P—— a couple off. So I told them all this s—— I was taking from them and after I told them that they were like, "Oh, man, I'm sorry. . . ."

T: Do you find that your friends respect you more?

C: They give me more respect in the sense that they don't always ask me to go all over hell for them. They don't expect me to do the simplest things that they can do themselves. Because I told them "No" and I told them why I said "No." They give me more respect in that sense. I give rides every now and again. Now instead of me always being the one who drives around, sometimes my buddies come over and pick me up if they want to hang out, and they drive me around. It ain't that often, but I mean, it's like either going to be that way or no way if you want to hang out. Now I stay home more, where before I always wanted to go out and do stuff; and don't get me wrong, I still go out but now I'm calling the shots of where and when and like with who, anything, but . . .

T: It sounds like you've been spending a lot of time doing these kind of Dr. M. things. You told me, too, you didn't care too much about school. Taking charge over you, you find that you have a more positive outlook on school now?

C: Um . . . So far in school, I've been doing all my schoolwork. I'm getting like A's and B's in all my classes. I've been doing a lot better since I am not driving everyone all over hell and back. It's like I actually do my schoolwork on those days when I'm supposed to, instead of listening to my friends saying, "Let's go and do this, or let's go and do that."

T: In the past when you were so concerned with your friends, how did that affect your schoolwork?

C: Well, it wouldn't affect some of the classes, because there were classes where I always got my schoolwork done in school. But for like the big classes and stuff when you always have homework, I would never be able to do it because my friends were over and they were like, "Well, do it at school tomorrow. Let's go out and have fun tonight." And I would listen to them and say Okay. Then I'd never get it done. And none of them ever got it done, so I'd never get my homework done.

T: So what's different about you now? How come you go to school, and . . . ?

C: I want to graduate, I got to do it for myself The whole reason why I'm doing it is for myself. I want to prove something to myself, too.

T: And how does that make you feel about you?

C: It makes me feel a lot better to know that actually I can do some good stuff in school. A lot better, because I always thought I was kind of illiterate. I didn't know what was wrong. I know I just never put effort towards it.

T: It sounds like you have more self-confidence now. You don't put yourself down, you don't think yourself dumb or stupid. You can see where it's not that hard. You've taken charge, you're doing it. You're getting A's and B's. It sounds like you're succeeding, therefore feeling better about you . . .

C: Yeah. I'm succeeding, not only in school but in other stuff . . .

T: So by giving up this idea that it's so important what other people think about me, and I've got to bend over backwards to please them, you've come to terms with that, and found out . . . you're finding out you're doing things to please you first. And again, how does that make you feel?

C: It makes me happy. That I can do the stuff that I want to do instead of the stuff other people want me to do. No one ever liked that. Seems like the car had a major role in all of this—I was the first one with a car. And since I was the first one with a car, everyone wanted to get a ride with me, because wow, man, if you can ride in a car, why walk? So they'd all be calling me and asking to hang out and then things just never ever changed. All my friends never got cars, they just kept getting rides from me. I got sick of it; and I go, Okay, I've had enough of it, you guys can get your own rides." Then they would like say, "Well, I want to hang out with you, man." Then me, "Oh really, you want to hang out with me or is it my car you want to hang out with?" But they wouldn't say anything, they'd *be* p——— off at me, but they wouldn't want to go home. They wouldn't talk to me, but they'll ride around in the car. And I didn't have enough heart to take them home.

T: But now . . .

C: Now, f——— 'em I'll drop them off right where they are. If you have a problem with me, man, my car is part of me. Now it really p——— me off. And I'll tell them the way it is and will be.

T: Doesn't that sound kind of selfish?

C: Yeah, it does kind of sound kind of selfish, but oh well. What you told me before, like there's this good kind of selfishness where it is Okay to put yourself first over others.

T: Aren't you happier with you? Listening to you and listening to what's right for you . . .

C: It's kind of selfish in a way, I guess, but it makes me feel a hell of a lot better. And if that's what having to be selfish has to be about, than so be it. I really feel happy about myself. I really feel proud of myself.

T: When you thought it was so essential that they like you, that you drove them here and there and everywhere, did it really make you feel good doing those kinds of things that you thought pleased them?

C: I felt like, kind of happy that I pleased them for a while, then towards the end, it just started to p—— me off and the more I felt used, the more it p—— me off; and I never did say anything because I didn't want to p—— them off, but it kept p—— me off.

T: "Because if I p—— them off"—what were you fearful of?

C: That they wouldn't want to be my friends no more.

T: And how would that make you feel?

C: Bad.

T: Would it made you felt rejected, worthless?

C: It would make me think all my fears were coming true. That all the time they were hanging with me and, like, using me for my car. And that's what I always thought to myself. But I didn't really want to like find out so I just kept it to myself till I'd had enough of it one day.

T: What's it like taking charge over yourself now? You're doing better in school, you're more confident, you can say "No" to them. You now have the time to visit your grandma and grandpa, your stepmom. Tell me more of what all that feels like.

C: It feels like I'm taking more control of myself; more responsibility for my own actions. Not so much for others who make me feel happy. I'm glad I did it. I'm glad I finally can do it.

T: Can you hear other sentences going off in your head now?

C: F—— 'em.

T: F—— 'em? "F—— 'em" isn't an all bad sense, is it?

C: No, no, in like the sense of screwing them over, like you don't screw over nobody. But f—— 'em.

T: F—— 'em in the sense that . . . ?

C: Who cares? I mean if they have a problem with me going out with my girlfriend or going out with my family when all they want to do is just go out and have a good time at my own expense, with my money for gas and all this other stuff, then they could walk. They can do whatever they want; I'm just not going be there as their go-boy. If I do go there, I'll show up later after I get done with what I wanted to do for that day. Any problems . . . too bad.

T: So the main changes in your thinking seems to be an initial thought of, "I must have people like me, I've got a car, they need me, I'm liked." You see where that finally took a toll, you were spending a lot of time and money pleasing them. Resenting that, you finally bottomed out, you took charge over you, and basically, as I've said, how much better that makes you feel. You're more confident, more self-assured, you find out that they haven't really abandoned you. As a matter of fact, as you said, it sounds like they respect you more now, because you're standing up for what's right for you.

C: True. That's exactly what happened.

T: So you like this more and more.

C: Yeah, I've liked it ever since the first time I did say "No."

T: You kind of took power over you . . .

C: At first, when I said "No," I was in shock. When I thought about it, I was like, "Wait a minute. That means you're not coming with me and that means I can still do what I was supposed to do." So that made me a lot happier after I said "No." That first time I said "No" it kind of like worried me a little bit. But I think you get a lot happier in the long run.

T: Where do you see this going now? The more you listen to you, listen to what's right for you, listen to the healthier sentences and voices inside of your head. Where do you see this taking you?

C: Further . . . for myself like . . . just happier. That's the only thing I can think about. I think it will make me a lot more happier, and I will feel better about me.

[AE: *Apparently the first two sessions Tom Mooney had with Jack really paid off. As a result of them, he saw his dire* need *for his friend's approval, saw that he was utterly miserable without approval, saw that his musturbatory thinking led to his* need— *and resolved to surrender his* need *and stand up for himself. He consequently devoted much more time to his family and his school work, which he had previously neglected.*

In this session, the therapist goes over in detail Jack's changed Beliefs and consequent improved behaviors. He makes sure, using detailed REBT questioning, that Jack is really changing his thoughts, feelings, and behaviors, and thereby solidifies his client's advances.

One important point could have been made more clearly by Dr. Mooney. The therapist notes, "You're getting A's and B's. It sounds like you're succeeding, therefore feeling better about you." Jack answers, "Yeah." This is inaccurate on the part of both Jack and the therapist. *Normally, the REBT goal is to have Jack succeed and to feel better about his* success, *not about* himself *for succeeding. As it stands, he has* conditional, *not* unconditional, *self-acceptance.*

Again, Jack says, in regard to his feeling "a hell of a lot better" about being selfish, "I feel happy about myself. I feel proud of myself." Not so good! In working with REBT, we hope that Jack will be proud of his newly found sensible self-direction (a behavior), not proud of *himself (his totality or essence).*

Jack's final words in this session, in answer to Tom Mooney's question, "Where do you see this taking you?" are "Further . . . for myself like . . . just happier. That's the only thing I can think about. I think it will make me a lot happier, and I will feel better about me." It would be preferable if he felt happier about his progress, *not* about *himself. Conditional self-acceptance again!*

Tom Mooney would have helped Jack more if he clearly showed him the difference between liking his new independence, but not therefore liking himself. Otherwise, he seems to have done a great therapeutic job with Jack.]

[JW: *It's impossible to know, but it may be that Tom Mooney was primarily focused on reinforcing the new Beliefs Jack had about his dire need for his friends' approval. That might be why he chose not to dispute Jack's conditional self-acceptance.*

I have been in sessions in which I tried to do "too much, too soon." Rather than helping clients build on the progress they have made, I've moved ahead too quickly.

Three sessions ago, Jack had no idea that it was his thoughts *about his friends' approval that were causing him to experience upsetting emotions. He now seems not only to understand this premise, but is behaviorally acting on it. Perhaps Dr. Mooney was taking his time and strengthening the gains before focusing on Jack's conditional self-acceptance.*]

References

Harris, J. R. (1998). *The nurture assumption.* New York: The Free Press.

Pollack, W. (1998). *Sacrifice of Isaac: Toward a new psychology of boys and men.* Paper presented at the Annual Convention of the American Psychological Association, San Francisco, California, August 1998.

An 8-Year-Old Boy Struggling With Perfectionism

Therapist: Ann Vernon, Ph.D.

This case study illustrates the application of REBT with an eight-year-old boy who had been referred for counseling by his parents and teacher. As a third grader, Phillip had issues relating to perfectionism that often resulted in anxiety and self-downing. He also frequently became frustrated in his attempts to be perfect, and this resulted in temper tantrums both at school and at home.

THERAPIST: Hello, Phillip. It's good to see you again. How is your summer going?

CLIENT: Oh, fine.

T: What's been happening since the last time I saw you?

C: Well, I got two trophies from softball.

T: You did? I bet you felt proud about that. What were the trophies for?

C: Well, one was for first place in tournament, and the other one was for, hmm, I can't remember what it's called.

T: For your team or for you individually?

C: For my team.

T: For your team. Well, that sounds pretty great. Congratulations!

C: Thanks.

T: Now if I remember right, weren't you upset a few weeks ago because you thought you weren't doing very well in softball? What does getting some trophies mean about that?

C: Well, that means I must be pretty good.

T: That's right. Was that a surprise for you?

C: No, not really.

T: No? But at the time that you were talking to me about this a few weeks ago, I think you were putting yourself down because you thought you'd made some mistakes in softball. Am I right?

C: Yes.

T: And that's kind of like the problems we started talking about last year when you first started coming in because of some of the problems at school, right?

C: Hmm. I remember what the other trophy was.

T: What was it?

C: It was for sportsmanship.

T: Phillip, I think that's fantastic! What does that sportsmanship award mean? I mean, what does it mean to be a "sportsman?"

C: Just that you don't, hmm, that you don't really, hmm, do anything bad, like, if you miss a ball, like, throw down your glove and get all upset.

T: That's right. So you use sensible behavior; you don't get all upset and think, "Oh dear, I made a mistake and therefore I am a terrible player and I'll never be good again." You know what? I think it's pretty special that you got this sportsmanship award. Now, let's talk a little bit about how you can get that same kind of sportsmanship award in school next year as a fourth grader. Not that it would be a sportsmanship award, but an award in school for using sensible behavior.

C: Okay.

T: It sounds to me like you got the sportsmanship award partly because when you made a mistake, you didn't get all upset, and you didn't throw a temper tantrum, and you didn't think a lot of negative thoughts, right?

C: Yeah.

T: So let's talk about then what you can do in school as a fourth grader, okay? Help me remember how you behaved last year when you didn't display good sportsmanship behavior in school. What did you do when you got upset?

C: Well, I'd just throw a big fit.

T: That's right. And you were throwing a big fit because what was going on in your head? What were you thinking to yourself?

C: I was thinking, since I didn't do this good, I'm no good at anything.

T: That's right. That is absolutely right. And you are kind of thinking [one] of the things the sportsmanship award showed you is that you don't have to be perfect at softball to get some awards and trophies, right?

C: Hmm, I guess so.

T: Just kinda like in school, maybe? You don't have to do everything perfectly?

C: Yeah.

T: Like today, I was grading my students' tests, you know, and some of them missed six, and they still got an A.

C: They did?

T: They did, so they didn't have to be perfect to get an A. Well, let's pretend that I'm your fourth-grade teacher. But before we start, can you remind me what subject you got most frustrated with?

C: Hmm, well, pretty much math.

T: Okay, math. So I'm going to hand back a math paper and put math, page 101 at the top of the page. And let's pretend that there are ten problems on that page, okay? So we have problem 1, 2, 3, 4, 5, 6, 7, 8, 9, 10 (I take slips of paper and write the numbers on the pages. I then distribute them to imaginary clients and to Philip in this role play). I'm going to hand back this paper and I'm going to have number 1 be right, number 2 be right, number 3 be wrong, number 4 be right, numbers 5 and 6 be wrong, and numbers 7 through 10 be correct. So now I'll hand back this paper, and I want you to just pretend to act like you used to act when you get a paper back that wasn't perfect. Okay?

C: Okay.

T: All right, I'll pretend like I'm handing out a few other papers. Shelley, here's your paper, and Brian, here's your paper. Mary, here's your paper, and here's your paper, Philip.

C: How come I got those wrong? (Phillip stomps his feet on the floor, tears up his paper, and throws down his book.)

T: My goodness, Philip, what's the problem? What are you thinking?

C: I don't know how I got those wrong.

T: So you don't know how you got those wrong. You sound confused.

C: Yeah.

T: It seems to me like you were feeling angry, too, because you tore that paper up and threw it and your book on the floor. Are you saying to yourself that you shouldn't have gotten those problems wrong?

C: Yep.

T: So you're saying to yourself that you should have gotten every single one of those ten problems right? And what does it mean about you if you didn't?

C: That I'm stupid and dumb.

T: Does that mean you're stupid and dumb all the time, every day, in every single thing you do?

C: (nods his head affirmatively)

T: It does, so that every single day you can never miss any, otherwise you'll be stupid and dumb? Well, are you stupid and dumb in everything, or do you just think you're stupid and dumb in math?

C: I'm stupid and dumb in everything.

T: Well, let's just take a look at that. (I use a paper and pencil exercise to illustrate this point. I draw a large circle and put smaller circles inside and label them: math, reading, spelling, softball, etc.) So here we've got math and you think you're stupid and dumb in math. And let's say we have reading, spelling, softball. What else, what other subjects do you have?

C: Science, music, um . . . social studies.

T: Okay. What about phys. ed.?

C: Yeah, and art, too.

T: Anything else?

C: I don't think so.

T: Okay. So here we have this big circle with all these little circles inside. Take a look. Now, you think you're stupid and dumb in math, so we'll put a big X on that. Is there anything else you think you're stupid and dumb in?

C: All of them.

T: All of them? Every single one of them?

C: (nods affirmatively)

T: But I thought I heard you say you got an award in softball and that meant you were pretty good. So should we leave the softball one in here?

C: Sure.

T: Okay. So now does that mean that every single day in math when you miss one or more that you're stupid and dumb?

C: No, not really.

T: Not really. And aren't there some days when you do get them all right?

C: Yeah.

T: So if you get some right some of the time, you can't be stupid and dumb all the time in math, can you?

C: (shakes his head negatively)

T: So should we just put a small X on that circle instead of a big one?

C: Yeah.

T: Now let's talk about science. Do you always do poorly in science, all the time?

C: Not really.

T: No?

C: Except for one time.

T: Oh, one time. Wow. Well listen, let's pretend like there's a line here on the floor right here in front of us. Let's have this end be all the time and that end right down by the wall be never. All right? So I want you to think about the science, think about your last five assignments. That might be kind of hard to think back, but can you think about some assignments you had in science? And would you say you got all of them perfectly right, none of them perfectly right, or were you someplace along this line?

C: Along here. (points to a place on the line)

T: Okay. Well, get up and stand on the line and let me see where you are. So that's closer to getting them all right than getting them not right. Right?

C: Yeah.

T: So what does that tell you, Phillip?

C: It means that I'm pretty good in science.

T: That's right and we've already decided you're pretty good in math and pretty good in softball. So if we kept going through all these circles, do you think that maybe the conclusion we would reach is that you're pretty good in all these subjects most of the time?

C: Yeah.

T: Okay, but let's suppose that one day or two days, or maybe even for a week, you would blow it completely. Now, what do you suppose is the likelihood of that happening, that you would just get all F's for five days in a row?

C: I don't think that would happen.

T: No. But sometimes do you suppose that the more you worry about it, the more likely it is you won't do as well?

C: Yeah.

T: Why is that?

C: Because I'm worrying about it so hard that I can't think.

T: That's exactly right.

C: And then I might not get as many right.

T: That's exactly right. The more you worry, the more likely you are to get more wrong because you're so bothered about what it is you're trying to do, right? Yeah, I'm so bothered about thinking that I'm not gonna get all these right that there's not as much brain left to think about the problems. Right. Your brain gets all polluted with all that junky thinking.

C: Yeah.

T: Well, let's get back to that little role play we did a few minutes ago. Here you have your paper on the floor, and you were feeling angry and confused because you missed some problems and didn't know how you could have gotten them wrong. I could tell that you were angry because of your behavior—you threw your book on the floor and tore up the paper. Were you thinking "Oh, it's awful that I got three wrong and I should have gotten them all right and because I didn't that means I am dumb and stupid"?

C: (nods affirmatively)

T: Okay, now let me see if you can change your thinking. I'm going to give you the paper back, okay? And this time you're going to miss three again. But this time you're going to try to say some different things to yourself, okay? So I'm going to hand out the papers and we'll see how you act when you think differently. Okay, now here's your paper, Brian. And who else did I have? Mary, here's yours. Shelly, did I have a Shelly?

C: Shelly, yeah, Shelly.

T: That's my niece. Okay, Shelly. And here is your paper, Phillip.

C: Yea, I only missed three!

T: So this time you seem happy about missing three.

C: Uh-huh.

T: Well, it's the same situation, so what were you telling yourself that made you happy about it this time when you were so angry about it before?

C: Well, three is still an A, so I might as well just say okay.

T: What if three hadn't been an A? Would that have been the end of the world?

C: No, 'cause I could still get all the other ones A's and stuff and get a good grade still.

T: Maybe so. But let's suppose it isn't an A. What does that say about you? Does it mean you are a dumb, stupid kid?

C: Not really.

T: So is it really the end of the world if you would get a B?

C: No.

T: And why not? If you get a B, does it mean you will always get all B's in everything all the time?

C: No, probably not.

T: You're right; I doubt that that would happen. So let's suppose it's next year and it's fourth grade. How do you want fourth grade to be different than third grade?

C: I want to have a real good year.

T: Good. And what does having a real good year mean to you?

C: It means that my mom and dad don't put me in my room.

T: And why did your mom and dad put you in your room in third grade?

C: Because I got all mad and stuff about little piddly things.

T: What were some of those little piddly things you got mad about?

C: Like the math test that we did here.

T: Yeah, right. So you got all upset about things that maybe you didn't need to get all upset about, right?

C: Yep.

T: So if you could choose what you get upset about, which you can really do, is there something going on in your life now that's worth getting upset about, more than missing some problems on a math paper, for instance?

C: Not really, not that I can think of.

T: Well, that's good. So last year your parents got pretty bothered because you would get upset over little things. Well, what did you do when you got upset? That's maybe the key.

C: Uh . . .

T: When you got upset, did you just kind of walk away with a frown on your face, is that why they put you in your room?

C: No, I kind of made a big disaster.

T: Did you? How did you make a big disaster?

C: In school, I'd just interrupt everybody.

T: Kind of lost your cool then?

C: Yeah, I got a bad reputation, so I gotta make it better this year.

T: Have you seen any of the kids from your classroom this summer, Phillip, that you felt like you got a bad reputation with?

C: Not that I got a bad reputation with.

T: So it wasn't everybody that you got a bad reputation with?

C: Well, no.

T: But it sounds like you were feeling a little guilty and knew you shouldn't have acted the way you did. Well, you know, Phillip, you just needed to learn some new ways of thinking, feeling, and behaving, didn't you? And you needed to learn that you don't have to get so upset if you don't do everything perfectly. And now that you've learned that since we've been working together, you've got an opportunity to change that for next year. And from what you've said, it sounds like you have been doing pretty well this summer.

C: Yeah. Except for that one time with softball.

T: And what was it that was upsetting for you then?

C: That the coach put me in right field and I didn't think he should have.

T: So you were angry with the coach for putting you there, because . . .

C: Because I wasn't going to be good in right field.

T: But then you ended up getting a trophy, right?

C: Yep.

T: I'm just thinking back to what you said about wanting fourth grade to be different. If I was a fourth grader and you had handed this paper back to me and I'd gotten three wrong, if I was behaving sensibly and wasn't going to throw a fit, what would I do when I got the paper back and saw that I missed three?

C: The same thing that I did.

T: The first time or the second?

C: The second.

T: And what do I need to be telling myself so I can be cool about this?

C: Hey, you only missed three. You still got an A.

T: Well, but I wanted to get them all right. (At this point, we slip into a roleplay, with the client playing the counselor.)

C: It's still an A and you don't really have to worry about it. If it was a B, it would have only been a little worse.

T: Is a B a really bad grade?

C: No, a B isn't even really a bad grade, so . . .

T: So I can get a B and I'd be okay?

C: Yeah. So you shouldn't get all upset about it.

T: But I want all A's, because my brothers get all A's all the time.

C: Well, if you keep on getting papers like that, you will. You didn't miss that many.

T: Oh, really? But I think I should get them with everything right.

C: Do your brothers get them with everything right?

T: Well, sometimes they don't, but I still think I should be better than they are.

C: Are they older or younger than you?

T: They're older. They're really good in things.

C: But they have more experience and stuff than you.

T: You mean, you think that'll help?

C: Yeah. If you get more practice in and stuff.

T: Oh, okay. Maybe you're right.

C: Practice makes perfect.

T: It does? What if I make mistakes all the time though, then it's not perfect, is it?

C: If you get more practice, then it sometimes will be perfect.

T: Do I have to be perfect? Do I have to get everything right all the time to think that I'm an okay kid?

C: No.

T: No? So, you think once in awhile I could miss a few and I'd be okay?

C: Yes. So you don't have to worry about missing some.

T: Okay, but what if I get upset? You know, I'm going into fourth grade and I know fourth grade is a little harder than third, and what am I gonna do next year when I get a paper back like this and I start feeling upset about it? What can I do so that I don't lose my cool and make a fool of myself?

C: Well, you could, well, just not do it.

T: Not get upset?

C: Yeah. Not get upset.

T: Well, so is there something I could think about or something that would help me kind of remember to not get upset?

C: You could, uh . . .

T: 'Cause, you know, I kind of think that I'm dumb when I make mistakes. And I think that I shouldn't make mistakes.

C: Well, act like there is like a Nintendo game or something in your head and it zaps all of those bad thoughts.

[JW: This is a great example of why rational role reversal—which is what I call it when I assume the role of the client and the client becomes the therapist—can be such a powerful therapeutic tool. Phillip comes up with the idea of pretending there is a Nintendo game in his head with a thought zapper. Perfect! Phillip obviously has experience with Nintendo games, so he envisions a thought zapper to be used when he is upsetting himself with certain thoughts. Dr. Vernon could use that example in future sessions with Phillip.]

T: Oh, that's a good idea. Okay, well, I could try that. Yes, I could just kind of pretend like I've got a zapper around my head and then when I get those thoughts, like I'm dumb and stupid and I shouldn't ever miss any, I could just kind of zap those thoughts.

C: Yeah, I think that will work.

T: You know, a friend of mine told me that I could kind of pretend like there's a stop sign in front of my face and then, when I start to get angry and upset with myself, then I can look at that stop sign, then I can just think, "Stop. It's not the end of the world. I don't have to get everything perfect all the time." Then maybe I can calm down and not act real upset and throw my paper on the floor and everything like that. Do you think that would work?

C: Uh-huh, I've tried that and it works.

T: Okay. Well, Phillip, I'll stop pretending that I'm you. You did a good job being my counselor! We just kind of slipped into that, didn't we? So what do you think you've learned from what we've been talking about today, Phillip, that will help you in fourth grade, so that you don't have the same kinds of problems, getting upset like you did in third?

C: I've just learned how not to be upset and that you don't have to be perfect.

T: That's right. So now that you think you don't have to be perfect, but what if you went to the other extreme? I mean, last time, in third grade, you were way up here and you thought you had to be perfect. (points to the invisible line on the floor referred to earlier in the session) What if next year in fourth grade you thought, "Oh well, what the heck, so what if I get B's and C's and F's? It doesn't make any difference." What would happen? What do you suppose that would be like?

C: Well, that would almost be worse.

T: So, we shouldn't go to the other extreme and say, "I don't care at all."

C: No, stay right in the middle. (points to the line)

T: Right in the middle, or you could even be a little up there, but you don't have to say, "I have to be perfect all the time."

C: That's about where my brothers are.

T: Really? I thought they were way up there at the other end and never ever made a mistake. So you exaggerated a little bit about how wonderful and great they are.

C: Yeah. But I have a wonderful and great family.

T: You have a wonderful and great family, and I bet they think they have a wonderful and great soon-to-be fourth grader. And even if that child makes a mistake now and then, do you think it's necessary for him to get all upset and completely lose his cool and have these awful temper tantrums and have to go to his room because he made a few mistakes?

C: No.

T: No. Would he get the student award, like the sportsmanship award, if he did that?

C: No.

T: No. So maybe what you and I could do next year is that we can pretend that there is an award like the good student award. What behaviors do you think you will have to exhibit in school to get the good student award?

C: I gotta be right here. (points to the middle of the line).

T: Meaning what?

C: That I'm a so-so kid.

T: A so-so kid? Well, you're probably not just so-so, because you do pretty well on most of your work most of the time, right?

C: Right. I'd be right over here. (points to the line closer to the perfect end)

T: Yeah.

C: But not way over there. (points to the perfect end)

T: Right. And because you thought you had to be way over there all the time and told yourself that you weren't any good if you weren't, that's when you started to get real worried and . . .

C: And went back down here. (pointed to the opposite end of the line)

T: Yeah. And that's also when you threw the temper tantrums and got put in your room, because you lost control of your behavior, right?

C: Yeah.

T: So let's just review one more time. What do you have to keep telling yourself so you won't get as upset and angry if you make a mistake or aren't perfect?

C: That I don't have to get it all right all the time and I'm an okay kid.

T: Well, it sounds like you know what to say to yourself. I also think you have some good ideas to help yourself. I liked your zapper idea and I think you've got some good techniques that you can use. We'll get together right after school starts or maybe right before school starts to review again, and I bet you can have a good year. What do you think?

C: I think I'll have a good year.

T: I think so too. I think it would be a good idea to keep that zapper inside your head and practice reminding yourself that you don't have to be perfect. I'll check to see how that is going when I see you again!

[AE: *This transcript of a session with "Phillip" and Dr. Ann Vernon shows that REBT can be successfully used with an 8-year-old who is something of a perfectionist. Typically, Phillip accepts himself only when he does very well in school and in sports. When he does poorly—or even moderately well—he blames himself severely and sometimes throws a fit.*

Ann Vernon reminds Phillip that he has just won two trophies for softball, with one for sportsmanship—for not upsetting himself while playing softball. Now, she cleverly points out, he can win a sportsmanship award in the fourth grade he is about to enter by not having a fit and downing himself if he fails to do some test problems perfectly.

Phillip insists, as he commonly does, that if he misses some test problems, "I'm stupid and dumb in everything." Ann consistently tackles his overgeneralizing, as is done in REBT and in Alfred Korzybski's general semantics. She shows Phillip, using several specific examples, that he can often do well in one subject and poorly in another, and that he can also do well and poorly in the same subject at different times. As a therapist, she shows Phillip that he can always accept himself unconditionally—yes, with his poor behavior; and if other people put him and his reputation down, he never has to agree with them. Others, such as his older brothers, may do better than he but they, too, are hardly perfect.

With Ann's help, Phillip sees that his negative thoughts largely create his feelings and that he has the ability to zap those thoughts, just as if there is a Nintendo game in his head with a thought zapper in it that he can use. Ann follows up by suggesting that he can pretend there is a stop sign in his head and look at it to see that it's not the end of the world when he becomes angry at himself for being imperfect.

At one point in the session, Ann and Phillip slip into a role play with Ann playing Phillip, who misses three test questions, and Phillip playing Ann, who tries to calm Phillip down. Phillip does very well playing the counselor and shows how he can calm Ann (in actuality himself) down if he does poorly at school or at sports. He spontaneously says, "I've just learned how not to be upset and you don't have to be perfect." Great! That is precisely what Ann Vernon wanted Phillip to learn in the course of her session with him.]

An 8-Year-Old Bedwetter

Therapist: Albert Ellis, Ph.D.

This is an interview with an 8-year-old girl, "Cathy," who came to therapy because she is wetting the bed every night, and not only wetting the bed but hiding the wet bedclothes because she is terribly ashamed of doing the wetting. Her parents are quite upset about this, especially her mother, who criticizes her endlessly and can't get along with her at all. Her mother is a very severely disturbed woman herself—she almost certainly suffers from borderline personality disorder, has never gotten along with her daughter, and keeps criticizing her for the bedwetting. In addition, probably partly encouraged by the mother, Cathy's four brothers and sisters also tend to tease her about the bedwetting. And friends—school friends and others—know about it and tease her, and she's very upset about this. Her father, who was also a severely disturbed person but has had several sessions of therapy with myself and is no longer as seriously disturbed, is the only one who sympathizes in the least with the patient. He is not around the house very much and is often separated from the mother, and consequently the mother continues to have her pernicious effect.

In the first two sessions of therapy, the patient primarily related how disturbed she was. Feeling that she was very bright and that there was an outside chance that REBT might work with this client, I started to use it; I began to try to reeducate her to show her that it didn't make that much difference if others teased her. What great difference did it make anyway? What could they really do to her? So I showed her, in very simple English, that if she stopped being so concerned, stopped taking others too seriously, that she would not get so upset, and if she didn't get so upset, there was a good chance she would stop her bedwetting. The client seemed to understand all of this, but naturally, being only an 8-year-old child she found it very difficult to put my techniques into effect.

This is now the third session and I am still continuing along the same REBT method, trying to acclimate the patient to the fact that there are people like her mother who severely criticize her, but she needn't take them too seriously even though she is an 8-year-old girl and these people often have power over her. I also clearly explain to her that her mother is disturbed and that Cathy is not to take the mother too seriously in the sense of getting hurt by her, although she often has to obey the mother's orders. In this session, rather to my surprise, Cathy starts giving me back some of my original coping statements to her, and I can see quite clearly that she does understand and she is trying to some degree to put them into effect.

CLIENT: She couldn't use it. I said, "Well, why don't you use it now because I'd like to have it." She said, "Oh, you be quiet." So she started calling me names because I wet and you know it made me real mad and I guess I lost my temper.

THERAPIST: Why did it make you feel mad when she called you those names?

C: I don't know.

T: You said that it's terrible to be wetting?

C: Yeah, I know.

T: But it isn't terrible. It's perfectly normal. Lots of children do it. Why is it so terrible? What are you so ashamed of?

C: I didn't feel like telling any of you because I felt ashamed that I am going on 9 and I am still wetting.

T: But that's probably why you're doing it, because you are so ashamed. If we could get you unashamed of it and relaxed about it, you wouldn't do it. Whenever a person is ashamed of a thing, they often keep doing it over and over. There is nothing to be ashamed of anything you do. Why should you ever be ashamed?

C: I don't know. It just to seems to me that I am ashamed because I am wetting and 8 years old.

T: Ashamed means you're telling yourself it's terrible to be wetting, to be doing this thing, and it isn't terrible. Not terrible at all. It's a nuisance. You can say that, but it's not terrible. And if anybody knows about it, that's not terrible, even if they laugh or they tease you or something. None of that is terrible.

C: But when I am called names like that, it just makes me think of it, and then I can't get over it and it makes me all nervous and jittery.

T: I say you can get over it. I say you don't have to think of it in the nighttime if you only won't take the names seriously. That's what makes you jittery. You're saying, "They shouldn't have called me those things. That's awful." It's just names.

C: I don't know how to get over that.

T: By stopping taking the names seriously. Not giving much of a damn what they think; not caring too much about what they say.

C: But that's kind of hard for me to do.

T: I know it's hard for you to do, but unless you do it you will go on being upset. That's what makes you upset—caring too much what other people think. It's not *that* important what they think.

C: I know. Any time they call me names, well, they don't care. They like to make me nervous or tease me.

T: That's right. Other children try to tease you because they want you to get upset. But why should you get mad? This is the way they are.

C: I know.

T: But you are not *accepting* them the way they are. You are saying, "They shouldn't be that way. They shouldn't tease me." And they do. The world is full of people . . .

C: I know, but I care and deep down it hurts me.

T: That's because you still believe that it is *terrible* what they think. *That's* what hurts.

C: I know and I tried it once before and it didn't work.

T: Yeah, but you still believe it's terrible and that's what you have to convince yourself over and over—that it's not terrible what people think or whether they laugh or whether they tease. No matter what others do, it's not *terrible*.

C: I know it's not terrible.

T: No, you think it *is* terrible. That's what hurts you.

C: The names hurt me.

T: Because you think the names are terrible. If you didn't care, if you were like me, people could call me names all the time. I don't care.

C: I know but you're used to it.

T: That's right, because I tell myself over and over, "Who cares? What difference does it make? I don't give much of a damn. It doesn't matter." And let me tell you something, nothing matters *too much*.

C: I know but it matters to me a lot.

T: That's why you're upset. I just spoke to a girl over the telephone and she told me that "I went away to this meeting last week and people were talking about you, Al, and many of them said bad things about you." And I didn't get upset at all.

C: Yeah, probably you didn't get upset because it didn't happen to you.

T: No, they were talking behind my back. She told me they were, and lots of times I've heard people talking badly about me to my face. It doesn't matter. I say

"Who really cares? Who gives too much of a damn? What difference does it really make?"

C: A couple days ago I just got so mad that it won't go away.

T: Because you said, "It makes a great difference. It's *awful*. It's terrible what they're doing!"

C: It really hurt me and I remembered all those names, and I was calling the kids names. It made me so mad.

T: It hurt you because you said, "They *shouldn't* be calling me these names. That's *terrible*." That's why it hurt you. Not because you remembered the names. Because you said, "It's terrible. It's *awful* they called me those names. How could they do that to me?" That's what's hurting you. And it's never *terrible*. It's never *awful*. It doesn't mean anything. That's the thing you've got to believe. You don't quite believe that. You believe that it is awful instead of it's *not* awful.

C: I remember a long time ago I felt good for quite awhile and then it started up again. I've stopped lots of times before because I'm not nervous, but sometimes I drink a lot of water, and lots of times I don't drink anything at all and I still wet.

T: The main thing that makes you nervous is caring too much what they think and caring too much about wetting. It wouldn't bother you whether you wet or not if you just say, "Well, that's too bad. So I wet tonight. What great difference does it make?" After awhile your worry would get less and less. But you've got to convince yourself that it doesn't matter that much. As soon as you worry about it, you'll get nervous and wet more.

C: I know. My mother doesn't approve of it very much and she gets mad and sometimes she'll yell at me.

T: That's right. That's the trouble. I've tried to get her not to get mad but she has her own problems.

I had one therapy session with her mother but she hardly listened to me and kept complaining about Cathy and about Cathy's father.

C: It makes me nervous and it makes me cry a lot. It's just that I feel so unhappy. I don't know why though.

T: It's because you take others too seriously. You say, "My mother is mad at me. That's terrible." That's what makes you unhappy. If my mother gets mad at me, I don't care that much.

C: The other day my brother started a fight with me and started hitting me and it made me nervous and I started crying. I felt so ashamed of myself, just letting him hit me and not going and beating him up. I felt so ashamed of myself.

T: Why? See there it is again. You're ashamed.

C: I don't know why.

T: Because you're saying, "It's terrible that I wasn't doing the right thing. I *should* have beat him up." Now we all make mistakes and maybe you made a mistake then but why is it so terrible when you make a mistake? What difference does it really make?

C: No difference.

T: But you *think* it does. That's what shame is. The only people who get ashamed are those who think it makes a great difference. And it doesn't make that much of a difference if you make a mistake. And you do make mistakes. I make mistakes. We all make mistakes. But when I make mistakes I say, "That's too bad. I'll try to do better next time." And you say, "Well, oh my God. Look what I did! This is terrible! I did the wrong thing." And that's what hurts you.

C: Yeah, well, it doesn't bother me at school. I guess.

T: Right. That's a very good point. In school you can make mistakes but when you do it with your brother you get terribly upset.

C: I get upset sometimes in school when kids start things to hurt me.

T: But you take them seriously. Nobody can hurt you.

C: I know, unless I let them.

T: That's right. Unless you let them. And you're letting them. You're taking these little things seriously, instead of saying, "They got their problems. They're crazy in the head lots of times."

C: Sometimes I feel that I'm crazy in my head.

T: That's because you take people seriously. That's what being crazy means. Crazy people are those who take things too seriously—who exaggerate the importance of things. They think things are very, very important when they are not. That's what crazy people are. Anybody who thinks a thing is very, very important when it's only of minor importance is crazy. And you go crazy, you get crazy, when you think that things are too important. When you calm down, you say, "What difference does it make? Who cares that much?"

C: Yeah, that's the thing that I've got to learn is to calm down.

T: Then say, "What difference does it really make?" That's what calm people say.

C: I know.

T: And calm people say, "All right, I did wrong. Better luck next time. Next time I'll try again. I'll do differently." They don't say, "Oh my God, I did wrong. I did wrong. I did wrong." Because then they'll never be calm. They keep their eye on next time instead of the last time. You never can change the last time. This business with your brother, you can't do it over. You already did it.

C: It's not only my brother.

T: Anybody else?

C: It's my sisters.

T: All right, your sisters, too. So what. Why do you take your sisters so seriously?

C: I don't know.

T: Why do you care so much what people think of you?

C: I don't know.

T: Because you were taught to, because your mother does. Your mother cares too much and you care too much. Most people care too much. If they're taught wrong, they care too much about what others think and they get very upset. Very intense. I used to care too much what people thought of me and I was very unhappy. Then I stopped caring that much and said, "What difference does it make? Who cares? So they don't like me. So I'll find other people."

C: I know, but sometimes I get so deep down into someone like Kim. I am so deep down into her and I like her so much that when she gets mad at me I just can't forget about her.

T: Yes you can. Yes you can. You can say, "She'll calm down. She's mad at me today. She'll accept me tomorrow."

C: I know she'll calm down. It's just that sometimes she really loses her temper and she then doesn't get over it for a couple of days.

T: So, she won't like you for a couple of days. Now why is that so terrible?

C: Well, it bothers me . . .

T: No, you bother you.

C: Because it makes me nervous . . .

T: You make yourself feel nervous.

C: And I feel bad that it is happening and it just seems to be like that.

T: It's too bad things like that happen but why should you get so upset? If she's going to go on a temper tantrum for two or three days and not talk to you, that's too bad.

C: And then I go and try to apologize to her . . .

T: Right.

C: Except she doesn't pay any attention to me.

T: That's right. So you'll have to wait for two or three days.

C: But it makes me nervous.

T: No. You make you nervous by taking it seriously. You don't have to take it so seriously. You could laugh it off and say, "That poor girl. She's not going to speak to me for two days. Isn't that sad for her. She gets so mad at me." And if you really saw how sad it was for her, then you wouldn't get so upset. You're saying, "Poor me. She's not going to speak to me. I won't get what I want for two days. That's terrible." That's what gets you upset. Nothing is terrible. It's too bad. It's not *terrible*.

C: I don't know if I can do it.

T: You can do it. It takes time. Don't be impatient.

C: It's hard.

T: Yes. Especially at your age. Most people don't do this in their whole life. They could be 50 or 60 years old and I am still teaching them not to care that much what other people think. I have clients ten times as old as you are, almost. One woman is 78 and she still hasn't learned, and she's a very bright woman, not to care that much what other people think. So don't be surprised if it takes you time. Don't be surprised if it's hard. These other people have it even harder than you.

C: I know.

T: And you can do it. I'm sure you can.

C: I can if I try very hard. I know.

T: That's right. You can learn not to care so much what other people think. No matter what they think or what they say. How they laugh. How they tease. You can learn not to care. You can tell yourself, "That's too bad. That's the way they feel. But what can they do to me by laughing or leering?" Nothing. If you really believe *that* you'll never get too upset about it. You'll get excited. That's fine. But you won't get too upset. You won't care that much about what other people think. Most people care too much.

C: Like me.

T: Yes, like you. That's right. You're normal. Most people are that way. I have to teach them. Like I said, I have clients that are 30 or 40 or 50 years old that I'm teaching not to care too much because they've been upset all their lives.

C: I'm a lot better than when I was littler.

T: Yeah. You've been upset for awhile taking people too seriously.

C: I know. Too, too seriously.

T: You don't have to.

C: I know that. It just seems that I do.

T: Because you're used to it. That's why. You've just done it so long that you're used to it. But you've got to fight it and fight it and fight it until it goes away. Just as if you played the piano wrong. It's quite hard to play it right.

C: That doesn't matter to me.

T: But it takes awhile to learn to play it right. It takes time, doesn't it?

C: Yeah, of course.

T: You've got to practice and practice. That's what you've got to do here. You got to practice not taking people seriously.

C: Yeah, I know.

T: It takes quite awhile, especially when someone is as young as you are. It's difficult at your age. You're a very young girl and it's very hard for people as young as you to do this but I still think you can do it.

C: I know I can, too. It's just that I got to get over it.

T: Get over taking people so seriously.

C: Let's see if I can do it again.

T: Okay. You go try again. Keep trying. You can do it. When they tease you, when they laugh at you, when they fight you, when they don't like you . . . whatever it is you just say to yourself, "It doesn't make that much difference."

C: To me it does.

T: But only because you're saying that it does. You're convincing yourself that it does. That's exactly the point. Now you have to convince yourself that it doesn't make that much of a difference. Because it doesn't. So they tease you. So what? They'll stop teasing you. So this girl doesn't speak to you for a day or two. Then she speaks to you again. In the meantime, you can get along very well without them. If you *think* you can, then you *can*.

C: I know I can too but it's hard.

T: It's hard because you're used to taking them seriously.

C: Yeah.

T: You're used to getting upset. You want them to like you and that's fine. But they don't *have* to. You can still be happy even when they're teasing you and even when they're not liking you.

C: But it will take me quite a long time, I think, to get over Kim. I've known her practically since I started school.

T: Yeah.

C: I've known her so long and she's been my best friend.

T: Yeah, well, we want you to like her but not care too much when she doesn't like you. We're not trying to get you to dislike her. You can like people. I like people lots of times, and when they don't like me back I say, "Well, that's too bad." And then I keep persisting and usually they like me after awhile. We're not trying to get you not to like her. You can like her very much. But when she doesn't like you for the moment, temporarily, you just say, "That's too bad. I'm going to live until she gets over it. It's not going to kill me." And it won't kill you.

C: I know all that.

T: Right. It would be nice if she didn't dislike you for a day or two but she will from time to time. She has her own problems and she's going to get very angry and dislike you. Lots of people dislike me. But I say, "Who cares? They'll come around. They'll like me tomorrow or the next day or the day after. Why do I have to care right now?"

C: I don't know.

T: You don't have to.

C: I know that.

T: You have to believe it. You know it but you don't believe it.

C: Yeah.

T: Yeah. You got to believe that it really doesn't matter what they say.

C: I have to learn to believe besides just knowing it.

T: That's right.

C: I have to work on it.

T: Oh, you work on it and you'll be surprised. It gets better and better. You got to learn to believe that teasing doesn't matter. Laughing at you doesn't matter. People not liking you doesn't matter that much. Even when they hit you it doesn't matter that much. They don't hurt you that much. You don't have to be too unhappy when these things happen.

C: You know that saying is true about sticks and stones.

T: That's right. Sticks and stones may break your bones but names will never hurt you. You've got to believe that more and more and more as you grow up.

C: Until I forget it.

T: Yeah.

C: And that's the thing I'm hoping.

T: Right. To forget your pain. You'll forget your unhappiness when you believe that. Forget what these people say about you and say, "So what? You called me names. Who cares? What difference does it makes?"

C: *I* do until I learn not to.

T: That's right. You're absolutely right. You care until you learn not to, but you learned to care. There was a time when you didn't care this much. Now you care. You learned to care and if you can learn to care, you can learn not to care.

C: I just . . . I can learn it.

T: You can. I'm sure you can. It just takes time. Don't get discouraged. Don't get discouraged at all, because there's no doubt you can learn it.

C: I know I can learn it if I try hard. The only way to learn is if you try hard.

T: The only way you learn . . . It took me a long time to learn this. I used to be sensitive and get very hurt when people teased me or laughed at me. Now I just say, "That's too bad. That's their problem. What great difference does it make? Who really cares?"

C: My father says that if I learn this, then if my child had a problem I will know what to tell them.

T: That's right. You will exactly know what to tell them. Your child gets upset and you just say, "Look, Dear, don't get upset. Don't even take anybody too seriously. Don't even take me too seriously." Your mother gets upset easily and therefore she has taught you how to get upset.

C: Yeah, a little too upset.

T: Yes. You see, that's her problem. She gets upset too easily and therefore you're copying her in getting upset. You're imitating her. And you've got to let her get upset without your getting upset.

C: Yeah. That's what I have to learn.

T: Yeah. It's the most valuable thing you can learn in life—not to take others too seriously. Not to get upset no matter what they do, or think, or tease, or say.

C: I know now.

T: You do. Keep trying. You're doing all right. You're not doing badly.

C: I know.

T: It takes time. It's hard work.

C: Since I have come here I've stopped. . . . I used to have fights . . .

T: And now?

C: Now that I've come I've gotten a little better.

T: You need to take them less and less seriously.

C: I'll see if I can do it.

T: I say you can.

C: So do I, but it takes time.

T: You're working on it. You're a young girl. You're only 8 now, right?

C: No, I'm going to be 9 soon.

T: You're going to be 9. So you're still 8.

C: Yeah.

T: All right. So you have plenty of time.

C: Yeah, I know.

T: There are people who are 80 that still take others seriously. So you have plenty of time to learn.

C: Yeah, I know that. I just want to get over it.

T: You'll get over it.

C: I hope by the time I'm 10, I'll get over it.

T: Don't put any date on it, just keep working and working and you'll see you'll get less and less concerned. As you said, before you saw me you took things more seriously, now you take them less seriously. Every day of the week that goes by you'll take them less and less and less seriously.

C: I'll try it.

T: Especially on this bedwetting. Let's not worry about it. It will occur from time to time. So what. Who cares? What difference does it make? It doesn't matter that much.

C: I was ready to cry when I first told you I wet because I was so ashamed to tell anyone.

T: Now you're not that ashamed, are you?

C: No.

T: No. We'll get you less and less ashamed.

C: I am not ashamed to tell you because I know you.

T: Right, but you're going to be able to tell it to other people that you don't know.

C: I know a long time ago I remember when I was at school I didn't wet anymore. That was when I stopped but it started up again.

T: You were ashamed to tell people?

C: Yeah.

T: It's nothing to be ashamed of. It's nothing. It's a nuisance. A bother. But that's all. It's no crime. No horror. Not terrible.

C: It's terrible for me.

T: But it isn't. That's because you're *calling* it terrible. Because your mother used to say it was terrible, you've got this idea that it's terrible. And it isn't.

C: It's not terrible if I learn that it's not terrible.

T: That's right. You're exactly right. If you learn that it's not terrible, it's not terrible

C: If I learn that it is terrible, then it is.

T: That's exactly right. Exactly. We've got to teach you that it's not terrible and then you won't be upset. If you keep wetting, you won't get upset. Some children wet for a long time until 11 or 12 years of age. It's not terrible. It's not awful.

C: I know.

T: Then stop worrying. You know it but you don't accept it. You don't believe yet. You've got to believe it. You've got to learn to believe it.

C: I know.

T: Okay. Let me talk to your father. You keep working on it.

The fourth session with Cathy takes place in June 1959, 1 month after the third session. Usually she was seen only once a month, in part because she lives out of town and has to come quite a distance for therapy. In this fourth session she tells how, for the first time, she was able to use what I had previously told her and not take the teasing of others too seriously. She really didn't feel—even inside, as she puts it—too badly when they teased her. She's afraid that she may not be able to keep this up, this good business of not taking others too seriously, but she has done it for the past few days and I encourage her to think that she will be able to continue to do it, which she thinks she will. Then she goes in more detail into some business with her mother who paranoiacally accused her of butting her with her head when the mother was leaning over her. Later I discover from Cathy's father that, just as he thought, this was paranoid behavior on the part of the mother. Before finding this out, however, I show Cathy that her mother is quite probably very disturbed and that Cathy is able to not take her very seriously. Just as in the case of others, I point out that Cathy doesn't have to be upset because her mother acts in this fashion. I again am rather surprised, because even though the child is 8 years of age and is bright, she does seem to really be listening to what I say. She seems to be eager to come to therapy, is being helped, and has, at least at this session, managed not to be too terribly upset. Subsequent to this session, Cathy was not able to come for awhile but the father wrote a letter to the therapist saying that she was distinctly better and for the first time, for 3 days running, has been able to go without bedwetting. She still has her problems and is a difficult child but she is getting along a lot better, presumably as a result of these four therapeutic sessions.

T: Well, how are things with you?

C: Good.

T: What's been happening?

C: Not much now. I've gotten over some of the things that I've told you. All kinds of names that I've been called. I have been called a couple of names in the past few days and I just say, "It's too bad for them that they want to call me names." And you know, I just turn around and I think of something else. And even inside it doesn't hurt me anymore as much.

T: See, I told you that's exactly what would happen.

C: Except even though I have gotten over that, it doesn't help me with the wetting.

T: Yeah, because you're letting the names hurt you in that respect. You're still worrying about what other people will think about your wetting and that's what's bothering you.

C: Well, how come the other day my brothers were calling me names about I was wetting the bed and everything and I said, "So what. It's too bad they want to call me names. It's not very nice"? And I just turned around and it doesn't hurt me at all. But then in the nighttime I just wet.

T: That's all right. But if you keep really telling yourself that it's too bad they call you names, you will stop wetting. It takes awhile but if you really keep convincing yourself . . .

C: It only started a couple of days ago.

T: See.

C: Then I said, "Well, what do I care if they want to call me names? Let them call me names. It doesn't bother me anymore."

T: That's exactly right. Now if we keep you saying this and really not worrying about it and not worrying yourself about the wetting, then the wetting will stop. Once you really stop worrying about it—but you've got to do that for awhile. Two days isn't long enough.

C: Yeah. It's been only a couple of days.

T: That's right. It's just been a couple of days but if we keep you for the rest of your life not caring too much when people call you names . . .

C: It won't bother me anymore.

T: That's right. It won't bother you anymore. That's the problem. And you can do it. I told you, you could. You thought you couldn't do it but you can.

C: Why am I saying to myself that I can't do it? I know I really *can* do it. So, the day before it got started up, I stopped and I said, "I'm going to stop and I won't think about it at all. And Dr. Ellis tells me that I shouldn't worry about what names they call me. And mother tells me that when they started calling me names, "Don't worry about it. You've gotten over it a little bit." Because I don't worry about it as much and it doesn't hurt me as much anymore.

T: See. That's right. Now, why can't you *keep* doing that?

C: I don't know if I can but I'm going to try.

T: If you try, you can. There's no doubt about it.

C: Oh, boy. I just hope it works.

T: It will work but you've got to keep working at it, and you're doing remarkably well.

C: I am doing well compared to what I used to be.

T: That is right. Compared to what you used to be.

C: I used to be so upset.

T: And now you're not that upset, are you? Now you get less and less upset as you take these things less seriously.

C: Pretty soon I won't even have to take them seriously.

T: That's right. That's exactly right.

C: I'm learning.

T: Yeah.

C: I hope I can do it.

T: I'm sure you can. You've done it so far in the last three days. Now why can't you keep it up?

C: I think I can if I try.

T: That's right.

C: Oh, boy. Now I won't get teased anymore.

T: No. They'll stop teasing you when you stop worrying about it and you stop taking them seriously.

C: They know that I worry . . .

T: That's right.

C: That I worry and that's why they want to call me names. But if they think that I am not so smart, I'm going to start acting like I'm not worrying about it. So I started stopping.

T: And then they started calling you names less, didn't they?

C: Yeah.

T: See. That's what happens. But it doesn't matter how often they call you names as long as you don't take them seriously. As long as you say to yourself, "So what? So they're calling me names. What difference does it make? That's their problem. They want to call me names. That's their problem. It's not mine."

C: I get over all the other kids. It's just John.

T: Why don't you get over John?

C: It's just that he's so mean all the time.

T: But that's because Johnny is disturbed. He must be an upset boy. Isn't he?

C: Yeah, he's upset.

T: All right then, you have to make allowances for his being upset. You've got to say to yourself, "Poor Johnny. He's upset. Why should I take him so seriously?"

C: Yeah. I worry about so many other people because they're upset and then it upsets me.

T: That's right. That's exactly right. If you stop worrying about them, it will not upset you.

C: I just feel so sorry for them that they're upset and it makes me upset.

T: That's too bad. No, you shouldn't feel *that* sorry. They have to take care of themselves.

C: Yeah, I know that.

T: There's little you can do about taking care of them. You just be mainly concerned about yourself and then they'll go on being this teasing way and sometimes they'll stop being this way. But you're really getting the idea of it. I have patients much older than you who aren't doing as well as you're doing.

C: Oh, boy. I can't wait till when this is all over.

T: It will be over if you keep doing what you have been doing for the last three days. You really won't care that much what people think.

C: Yeah. If I keep it up.

T: That's right.

C: And I'm sure I'll keep it up if I really want to try.

T: That's right. You *can* keep it up.

C: I just hope so.

T: Are you out of school now?

C: Yeah.

T: So you're on vacation. All right. So you should really be enjoying yourself. How are you getting along with your mother?

C: I don't know. I'm not sure about that.

T: Is she yelling at you or anything?

C: No. But there's one thing I hate about her saying. Every time she thinks up some ideas that aren't even true. The other night she went to kiss me good night and she said that I was going to hit her. And I get so mad at her for saying that because I know it's not true. She says things that I don't even think of.

T: Yeah.

C: And she makes me so upset.

T: That's because you take your mother too seriously. Your mother has her problems, too, and I agree with you she is making this up. It's not true and she thinks it is true. Now, that's because she's so frightened. She's so fearful herself.

C: And she makes up so many ideas. She says that I jerked so that she would bang her teeth on something. And I got so mad at her. She's always thinking the wrong ideas and I get so mad at her for doing that.

T: Right. But she can't help it. Your mother is a disturbed woman. She really believes these ideas, even though they are untrue. And you have to make allowances for your mother and say to yourself, "My poor mother. She believes this and it's false. Now why should I get upset because she believes something that's false?"

C: I don't know. It's not that I get upset. Maybe it's just that I don't like her saying those things that aren't true about me.

T: Yeah.

C: I just don't like it.

T: Right. But there's nothing you can do to change people like your mother. They're very upset and they do these kinds of things and the world has a lot of these people in it. You know your mother best. But later on you're going to find lots of other people are like that. They make up things they believe are true and they're not true. So they accuse you of things unfairly, but what can you do?

C: Try not to think of them.

T: Yeah. You don't have to get upset because people accuse you unfairly. Do you?

C: No.

T: Nobody has to get upset.

C: I try.

T: Just make allowances for these poor people who think wrongly. They really believe wrongly.

C: But those are the only things I get upset over—wetting and my mother saying those things that aren't true.

T: Yeah. Well, but those two things are nothing to get upset over. The wetting will take care of itself. If you stop worrying about it, it will gradually go away. It will take awhile but it will go away. The less you worry about it, it will. But your mother saying things that aren't true is not going to stop. She probably is going to keep saying them because she's very upset herself.

C: She's been saying them a lot to me.

T: That's right. She'll probably keep saying them.

C: She won't stop saying them to me every time she thinks I'm trying to do something.

T: Probably. But she's probably wrong about you trying to do something. She just thinks you are. She's probably wrong. It's a shame.

C: Sometimes I think she says that because I think she doesn't love me.

T: No. I think she loves you but she's very disturbed. She's very irritated herself. She's so upset herself at times that she's going to act as if she doesn't love you. That's true. Because when people are so upset, they don't really love anybody right then. They are too upset themselves.

C: But when I tell my mother that you said I was upset because she was upset, she didn't believe me that she was upset. She said she doesn't get upset.

T: She thinks that, and you don't have to tell her what I said. Because between you and me, she's very upset. She just doesn't want to admit it. She's so upset that she doesn't want to admit it to herself. She doesn't believe she is, but she is.

C: She's very upset.

T: That's right. She's very upset and she doesn't want to face it. And it's no good telling these people they're upset, because they'll deny it. You have to tell yourself, "Yes they're upset." But you don't say it to them. Just like when you see somebody who's crippled, you don't go up and say, "Look you're crippled." You say to yourself, "That boy or that girl is crippled." But you don't say anything about it. Your mother is crippled mentally. She doesn't think straight. She's too upset. And that's too bad. She may get over it someday but not for a long time, I'm afraid. While she's crippled in this manner, while she's mentally upset, she's going to make up lies about you and she's going to believe them. She really believes these things. She doesn't realize that they're not true.

C: And I told her that I didn't jerk her arm to make her hurt herself and she said that I did do it.

T: Well, she *believes* you did. She really *believes* that. She's not making that up. She thinks you did. She's overly suspicious. Lots of people are. That's what one gets when one upsets oneself; and your mother is a very upset person. We have to get you not to take her too seriously, even though she is your mother.

And not to feel hurt when she lies. And that's tough to do but you've just got to do it.

C: Yeah, I know that.

T: Yeah. Because then you'll feel much better because you'll stop worrying about your mother and about the wetting. The wetting will go away and your mother will remain the same but it won't bother you.

C: I haven't been too upset about it.

T: See, you're getting less upset now. The less you worry about it the less you will wet.

C: Yeah, but the first time I came here to visit you and I told you about wetting I almost started crying because I was so ashamed of it.

T: That's right, but now you're not so ashamed are you?

C: No.

T: It's nothing terrible about wetting. Little girls do it often when they're excited and upset. And when they worry, they wet. When they get less excited and less upset and stop worrying about things, then they stop wetting. But it's no crime. There's nothing to be ashamed of. The less you take people seriously, the less upset you get, the less you will wet, but it takes awhile. It takes some time. You've got to get used to not worrying. You started in the last three days.

C: Yeah, but can I do it for all the rest of the days?

T: You can. If you can do it for three days, you can do it for three hundred days.

C: I hope.

T: No doubt about it.

In the first part of the third session with Cathy, I continue to try and show her that wetting her bed is unfortunate, but that it is not *shameful*. She doesn't have to put *herself* down because of this undesirable behavior. Consistently, during this session I keep trying to help her understand one of the primary therapeutic principles of REBT—namely unconditional self-acceptance. I give her unconditional other acceptance or what Carl Rogers calls unconditional positive regard. But I quite actively-directly persist in trying to teach her that she *can* choose to have unconditional self-acceptance and that having it will help her—first to feel unashamed of her bedwetting (just sorry and disappointed about it).

Second, I keep showing her that if she makes herself anxious and self-deprecating, she will most likely continue to wet the bed more. On the other hand, if she *dislikes* her bedwetting, but tells herself that she *absolutely must not* do it and that she is a *bad girl* for doing it, her self-created *panic* that stems from her musturbation will in all probability make her wet the bed more. During this session, I continue strongly repeating several rational coping statements to Cathy, as I have done during the first two sessions, hoping that she will accept them, make them her own, and decrease her self-downing and bedwetting. At first Cathy seems to parrot back my rational coping statements but, as the session goes on, she appears to start believing and acting on them.

At the same time that I try out some anti-shaming ideas with Cathy, I also try to convince her that although many things are bad and unfortunate—such as her mother, siblings, and peers criticizing her for her bedwetting—these bad events are not *awful* or *terrible,* only highly inconvenient. I try to show Cathy that she *makes* things "awful" by taking them *too* seriously or telling herself that people *must not* act the "unfair" way that they do act and that they are "rotten people" for acting that way.

I thereby keep making it clear to Cathy another very important REBT point—namely, that her and other people's feelings go along with their thoughts; and, therefore, her anger at her siblings and mother is partly created by her own *demands* that they *must not* behave the way they are "unfairly" behaving. Although Cathy is only 8 years old, I teach her, albeit in simple language, the same REBT principles that I teach to adolescents and adults: that they do not *just* feel angry, anxious, and depressed when they encounter Adversities. Instead, they significantly contribute to *making themselves* experience these disturbing feelings. If this is so, I explain to Cathy, she can make herself healthfully sorry and disappointed when others treat her badly, but not anxietize, depress, or enrage herself about their treatment.

To show that I am probably somewhat getting through to Cathy, early in this session she says, "I get upset sometimes in school when kids start things to hurt me." I say, as I have said before, "But you take them seriously. Nobody can hurt you." Cathy replies, "I know, unless I let them." Ah, my teaching is seeping through!

The therapist needs to be continually encouraging. I tell Cathy that it will be hard for her not to take people too seriously, and it will require time and effort until she reaches that goal. But I keep showing her she can do it. This kind of encouragement, which Alfred Adler espoused many years ago, is one of the emotive techniques of REBT and it is particularly useful when it is used in children's therapy.

As is often the case in REBT, I do not hesitate to use my personal life as an example. Thus, I show her, "I like people lots of times and when they don't like me back, I say, 'Well, that's too bad.' And usually I keep persisting and then they like me after awhile." I thereby use another REBT and CBT technique: urging clients to model themselves after myself and other people who refuse to upset themselves when bad things happen to them, and thereby get better results.

When I remind Cathy that it doesn't matter too much if she doesn't take criticism too seriously, she says, "You know that saying is true about sticks and stones." This shows that she is probably starting to believe what I told her a few times in the previous two sessions: "Sticks and stones will break your bones but names will never hurt you. Unless you sharpen them up and stick yourself with them!" Again, she seems to be learning how to refuse to upset herself about people's teasing.

I show Cathy that she partly learned to get very upset because her mother is upsettable. Of course, she may have her own biological tendencies, in addition to her socially learned ones, to be quite upsettable. If Cathy were an adult, I might explain this to her. But I think it best not to do so at this point. However, I prophylactically keep showing her that her mother, her siblings, and some other children have their own serious emotional problems. This is to teach her that many people are quite upsettable and that they sometimes criticize her strongly because of their *own* problems.

Cathy says that she was so ashamed that she started to cry the first time she told me about her bedwetting, but now she is not ashamed because she knows me. I point out that she can make herself less ashamed even with other people.

At the beginning of the fourth session, Cathy reports some remarkable progress in being called "all kinds of names" and not upsetting herself. But she still wets her bed at times. I assure her, because I actually believe it will work that way, that if she *keeps* worrying much less about her bedwetting and about being teased for it, she will most likely get over most of her bedwetting. Cathy also reports that when she worries less about name-calling, other kids do tease her less— as I predicted they would do.

Cathy then reports about her mother's paranoid behavior of making up things that aren't true. Without quite telling her that her mother is severely paranoid, I explain that she is mentally crippled—and that is why she thought Cathy deliberately tried to hit her when she leaned over to kiss Cathy goodnight. I tell Cathy that it's a shame that her mother will probably at times falsely accuse her of harming her. But if Cathy continues to stop upsetting herself, she will be able to handle her mother's odd behavior, as well as her own bedwetting.

After this fourth session, Cathy came once more a month later and reported consistent progress in not being bothered by being teased for her bedwetting or practically anything else. She had only wet the bed once during this month and was quite confident that she would rarely wet it again. Her father confirmed her progress and was enthusiastic about it. She was also getting along much better with her paranoid mother. Her father came to see me for several more sessions to work on his own problems, and he reported that Cathy was continuing to do very well, was not wetting her bed at all, and wanted to thank me for all the help I had given her. She didn't think she needed any more therapy at that time, and her father and I agreed with her.

SUMMARY

A common misconception held by many therapists who haven't been exposed to REBT beyond a chapter in a counseling text is that "REBT has to be done the way Albert Ellis does it." I (JW) met a school counselor who knew of my work with REBT, and after working together for a few weeks she confided in me, "I thought you'd be exceptionally direct." Dr. Ellis is the originator of REBT and certainly a preeminent therapist and author, but he has his own style—in fact, several styles, depending on what type of client he sees. There are many ways to adapt REBT to different styles. This book was designed to demonstrate some of those adaptations by presenting a variety of therapists using a range of techniques with children and adolescents.

Howard Young, a therapist I (JW) greatly admire, humorously and directly taught an adolescent with "parent problems" one of the many ABCs of REBT; namely, that the client *chooses* to upset himself at *C* (his angry consequences) by irrationally Believing (B) "they *shouldn't* bother me so much! I can't stand it!" In just a few minutes, Howard Young had the client understanding that *he and his Beliefs (B),* rather than his restricting parents *(A),* make him mad *(C).* He also helped the client adopt the new Rational Belief, "My parents may be wrong, but they are fallible people who have the right to be wrong!"

Marie Joyce, in a second session with Cara, *assumes* that the girl is right about describing her mother's unfairness and does not question her description. REBT holds that even if her mother *was* unfair, Cara would not have to choose to be very angry at her, but instead could merely make herself feel quite frustrated and disappointed, which are *healthy* negative feelings when something "unfairly" goes wrong in her life. So the therapist helps Cara see that she largely *made herself* angry at her mother and that she can also make herself healthily disappointed at her mother's *behavior* but not unhealthily incensed at *her,* the whole behaving *person.*

Dr. Joyce goes on to demonstrate the use of using rational-emotive imagery with Cara. She asked Cara to recapture the same angry feelings about her mother's behavior toward her. Once Cara signaled that she had re-created her angry feelings, Dr. Joyce asked her to change those feelings from anger to merely frustration. When Cara was able to accomplish this, Dr. Joyce asked her what she had done to create these new, less angry feelings. It was a nice example of how REBT therapists help clients access their own rational coping statement or learn new ones from the therapist.

Rod Martell's session with Beverly demonstrated the hypothetico-deductive "evolving" assessment strategy in which assessment, teaching, and therapy are intertwined in a multilevel dynamic "power" session. This type of assessment is often employed in REBT. The client stubbornly refused to give up the Irrational Belief, "I'm too fat, as I *must* not be, and my *fatness* makes me an inadequate and unlovable *person*." Martell attempted several rational ways of disputing these ideas.

He showed Beverly that she may well have a genetic disposition to easily gain and regain weight, so he indicated to her that she is by no means totally responsible for her fatness. This is a legitimate disputation but is somewhat inelegant, and she does not buy it and exonerate herself.

Martell explained that even if she was somewhat responsible for being overweight, she did not need to feel guilty or self-deprecating for being so. Finally, he used REBT to tackle Beverly's self-downing for her weight and for other people's disapproval. He valiantly tried to help her achieve unconditional self-acceptance. Martell pointed out that her *behavior* may be bad, but that never makes her a bad *person*. He rightly tried to help Beverly achieve unconditional self-acceptance, but it may take some time for her to do so.

Martell's case is a nice example of what I (JW) like to call "switching the *A*." Beverly kept bringing up new Activating events whenever Martell started to help her critically examine her thinking and her responsibility (ownership) for this problem. Thus, she brought up her grandparents' accidental deaths as Martell was starting to dispute some of her irrational thinking, and later in the session she switched the Adversity to her parents' behaviors.

Unfortunately (or fortunately), clients do *not* have the power to control other people nor do they have the ability to go back in time and relive earlier experiences. That is why helping them accept their role in their present circumstances *and* to accept their ability to change their thinking is so important. To a certain extent, their thinking, emotions, and behavior may be some of the few things they can control.

Jerry Wilde presented three sessions with a fourth-grade boy, John, who has anger problems. Dr. Wilde used the following sequence of activities for the first session:

1. Asked the client for an anger problem or a situation where he angered himself (i.e., identify and get the client to agree upon the Adversity *(A)*).

2. Asked the client to describe the disturbed Consequence *(C)*, his anger.

3. Explained that *A* does not by itself cause *C*. There is something more than that— the client's Belief system *(B)*.

4. Used "the blind man on the bus" story to illustrate that *B* largely causes *C*.
5. Moved the logic of "the blind man" to the problem John presented.
6. Helped John identify the Belief that is mainly leading to his anger.
7. Helped John change his Irrational Belief into a Rational Belief.
8. Gave an assignment to help John practice using his new Rational Belief.

By the second session, John seemed to do a pretty good job of remaining only irritated when the other players used swear words. The latter half of the third session was spent assessing his self-acceptance. Many students feel that if others don't accept them, they can't accept themselves. John did not appear to suffer from this dire need for approval, which was a positive indicator for his overall emotional development.

Thomas F. Mooney demonstrated the advantage of an REBT approach to issues of peer group influence by using its ABC model. Point *A* represented the client's peer group taking advantage of him. Point *B* was his Beliefs that he absolutely must have their approval. Point *C* was his anxiety of self-downing when he thought he lacked the approval of his peers. At point *C* he also gratified his peers at his own great expense. This particular session focused primarily on those sentences that the client was telling himself about how crucial and necessary it was that his friends like him and approve of him, resulting in his giving too generously of his time, his car, and his money.

Jack was helped by Dr. Mooney to see his dire *need* for his friend's approval, to recognize that he was utterly miserable without it, and to become aware that his musturbatory thinking that led to his misery. He resolved to surrender his *need* and stand up for himself. He consequently devoted much more time to his family and his schoolwork, which he had previously neglected.

Dr. Mooney explores, in detail, Jack's changed Beliefs and consequently improved behaviors. He makes sure, with detailed REBT questioning, that Jack is really changing his thoughts, feelings, and behaviors and thereby solidifies his client's healthy reactions.

Terry London introduced new ways for his client to think about his problems (or "rough spots"). London encouraged his client to learn how to become good at shrinking those rough spots down in his life. To become proficient in this respect, the client had to enable himself to do two things. First, he had to learn how to build emotional muscle or how to stay cool and not upset himself over the rough spot. Second, he had to make up a plan of attack to deal with it.

I (JW) liked London's methods of taking REBT principles and explaining them by using language that his client could easily understand. By the end of the client's sessions with London, the client wasn't going to be biting any hooks!

Ann Vernon demonstrated that REBT can be successfully used with an 8-year-old boy who is something of a perfectionist. Typically, Phillip accepted himself only when he did very well in school and in sports. When he did poorly, he blamed himself severely and sometimes threw a fit. With Dr. Vernon's help, Phillip sees that his negative *thoughts* largely create his *feelings* and that he has the ability to zap those Irrational Beliefs, just as if there is a Nintendo game in his head equipped with a thought zapper that he can use. Dr. Vernon followed up by suggesting that he could pretend there was a stop sign in his head and look at it to see that it's not the end of the world when he gets angry at himself for being imperfect.

At one point in the session, Dr. Vernon and Phillip role-played a situation in which the therapist played Phillip, who misses three test questions. Phillip played Dr. Vernon, who tries to calm Phillip down. Phillip did very well playing the counselor and showed how he can calm Dr. Vernon (actually himself) down.

Dr. Ellis's case with Joey, who was whining about dogs in his house, was a good example of what often happens when a therapist works with a child or adolescent. A good portion of this case was devoted to (a) getting a clear picture of the situation in the boy's home and (b) helping him try to develop a better plan for dealing with this annoying situation. Dr. Ellis gave him several ideas that might have minimized the problem, such as getting rid of one or more of the animals. As is often the case, the client gave reasons why those alternatives would not work. Dr. Ellis then tried to help Joey see that he was making the problem worse by his demandingness and his tendency to awfulize about the animals in his home. Near the end of the session, Dr. Ellis again tried to help the client think of alternative solutions, such as the possibility of a fence. As this session illustrates, sometimes the focus had better be on helping the client problem-solve.

Dr. Ellis presents the case of Cathy, an 8-year-old bedwetter, who was ashamed of being teased by her mother, siblings, and school friends about her problems. Cathy also had a paranoid mother who falsely accused her of deliberately harming her physically. This is one of the first cases where REBT was used successfully with children. It shows how Cathy finally was able to repeat back and to use Dr. Ellis's rational coping statements that he kept teaching her, to deal with her feelings of shame and anger, and how she was able to handle the tauntings of her mother, siblings, and other people. Despite her young age, in a few REBT sessions, Cathy learned to conquer some of her serious emotional and behavioral problems and to be a happier child.

Dr. Ellis's session with Mary, whose parents were separating, demonstrated how to help children handle a parent's angry outbursts and be much less resentful of a parent's "unfairness." Mary's father was enthusiastic about her changes and thought that they proved that REBT could work nicely for both him and Mary. Although Dr. Ellis had only one full session with Mary, he diagnosed her as being only moderately disturbed and tried to teach her three of the main philosophies of REBT: (1) to have unconditional self-acceptance, even when some of her behaviors—such as anger—were dysfunctional; (2) to learn to have unconditional other-acceptance even when people—like, again, her mother—were behaving poorly; (3) to gain high frustration tolerance when the conditions of her life were unfortunate. According to Mary and her father, Dr. Ellis was able to help Mary in all these respects.